THE SAT IS A TEST
IT IS *ONLY* A TEST

If it were an actual indicator
of your intelligence, you
wouldn't be able to prep for it.
But you can, and this book is
a great place to start.

KAPLAN
SOURCEBOOKS™

SAT*
IN A
WEEK

BY THE STAFF OF

STANLEY H. KAPLAN EDUCATIONAL CENTER, LTD.

Bantam Doubleday Dell

*SAT is a registered trademark of the College Entrance Examination Board, which does not endorse this book.

KAPLAN SOURCEBOOKS™
Published by
Bantam Doubleday Dell Publishing Group, Inc.
1540 Broadway
New York, NY 10036

Copyright ©1994 by Stanley H. Kaplan Educational Center Ltd.

All rights reserved. No part of this book may be reproduced or transmitted in
any form or by any means, electronic or mechanical, including photocopying,
recording, or by any information storage and retrieval system, without the
written permission of the Publisher, except where permitted by law.

Excerpt from "On Seeing England for the First Time": Copyright ©1993 by
Jamaica Kincaid. Reprinted with the permission of Wylie Aitken & Stone, Inc.

A Seth Godin Production
Design: Karen Engelman, Seth Godin, Julie Maner.
Editors: Gary Krist, Julie Maner.
Production: Megan O'Connor, Carol Markowitz,
Karen Watts, Jennifer Gulledge, Lisa DiMona, Chris Angelilli.
Copyediting: Jolanta Benal.
Cartoon: Holly Kowitt.
Thanks to Robert Leinwand, Richard Ticktin, Michael Cader.

Manufactured in the United States of America
Published Simultaneously in Canada

August 1994

10 9 8 7 6 5 4 3 2

Library of Congress Cataloging–in–Publication Data
SAT-in-a-Week/by the staff of Stanley H. Kaplan Educational Center Ltd.
     p.   cm.   (Kaplan sourcebooks)
     ISBN 0-385-31276-8
     1. Scholastic aptitude test--Study guides. 2. Universities
and colleges--United States--Entrance examinations--Study guides.
     1. Stanley H. Kaplan Educational Center Ltd. (New York, N.Y.)
     11. Series.
LB2353.57.S2675   1994
378.1'662--dc20

93-23315
CIP

From the day she was born, Emily's parents
knew she'd do well in school

CONTENTS

Preface: Is It Too Late to Prepare for the SAT?

Okay, maybe the dog ate your calendar. Or maybe your chemistry lab partner spilled hydrochloric acid all over your list of SAT dates. Or maybe — what with serving as president of your class, being captain of the football team, and editing the school newspaper — you just let the test slip your mind.

But whatever the reason, the fact remains: The SAT is just around the corner, and you aren't prepared.

So now what?

Enter Kaplan's *SAT-in-a-Week*, the book you're holding in your hand right now. Think of it as emergency prep, a first-aid manual for the last-minute preparer. Here, in this convenient little volume, are gathered just about all the most important things you need to know before walking in to the SAT. And all this information is laid out for you in fifteen easy steps, so that you can learn it over the course of a single week.

Now, don't get us wrong: This book won't give you comprehensive SAT preparation. After all, you can't build a perfect SAT score in a week, any more than you can build Rome (or even Little Rock) in a day.

But you *can* improve your test-taking habits in a week. You *can* gain the familiarity with the test you need to start racking up points. You *can* learn the basic skills, techniques, and strategies that will make you a better SAT taker.

In other words, you *can* boost your SAT score in a week.

How? By following the easy-to-use seven-day prep plan outlined below. We won't bog you down with long vocabulary lists and endless catalogues of math principles. You don't need that kind of in-depth study to improve your score. *You can boost your score by 100 to 150 points just by getting two extra questions correct on each section!*

So, instead of bombarding you with details, we focus your energies on the essential elements of the exam — places where you can really boost your score easily, and fast!

For instance, we've picked out the eight top math traps that appear again and again on the SAT. In a couple of hours, you can learn how to avoid these traps and improve your math score significantly. Similarly, we've developed some easy methods for figuring out the meaning of unfamiliar vocabulary words, so that you can pile up verbal points even if you've never heard of the words in the question.

So don't panic. No matter what your excuse for waiting this long — your evil twin stole your SAT registration form? — you can heave a sigh of relief. With *SAT-in-a-Week* in hand, it's not too late to get in some solid preparation for the SAT. If you've still got a week, you've still got a chance to boost your score.

The study program for SAT-in-a-Week is designed to be completed in seven days, requiring just one or two hours per day.

We've divided the material into 15 distinct "steps." Each day you'll be covering one or more of these steps, each centered around a different area of SAT techniques and tips. Feel free to skim the steps you feel confident of so that you can spend more time on the ones you feel shaky on. The 15 steps vary in length, but they're all important to your score, so make sure you at least have a look at each one.

The icon at the beginning of each step should help you keep track of how far along you are in the 15-step program.

Here are the other major components of the study program designed to make your training easy and effective:

THE STEPS

1. SAT Know-How
2. Format Orientation
3. Basic Math Strategies
4. QC Techniques
5. Basic Verbal Strategies
6. Analogy Techniques
7. Calculator Techniques
8. Classic Math Techniques
9. Sentence Completion
10. Critical Reading/Basic
11. Critical Reading / Focused
12. Math Trap Techniques
13. Grid-In Techniques
14. End-of-Time Techniques
15. Last Minute Tips

AT-A-GLANCE BOXES

At the beginning of every day's chapter you'll find a box titled "At-a-Glance." This box gives you a preview of what will be covered that day, with checkboxes for each of the major topics, so that you can check them off as you master them. If you decide to skip a topic and return to it later, leave the checkbox blank so that you don't overlook it. By the night before the test, each box should be checked. The At-a-Glance boxes also give you a recommended amount of time to spend on each topic.

QUICK TIPS

Scattered throughout each step are various "Quick Tips" — one-sentence summaries of the major tips and strategies covered in the step. It's extremely important that you learn these points, which is why we've set them off in the text. Also set off from the body of the text are various other hints, pointers, and speed tips that you should pay close attention to.

STEP RECAPS

At the end of each step, you'll find a box called "Step Recap." Here, to save you time, we've gathered together all of that step's Quick Tips in a single place. Review these recap boxes frequently to imprint these important points on your brain. You should also review these recaps at the end of your study program, a day or so before the test. If you remember nothing else on test day, remember these points.

POP QUIZZES

At the end of many steps there will also be a "Pop Quiz" testing you on the material covered in that step. Try to complete these quizzes within the time limits shown, which reflect the timings for these questions on the actual SAT. Part of the trick of doing well on the SAT is performing well under time pressure, so be strict with your stopwatch!

Using these four study aids will help you focus your time and energies so that you can get the best possible score improvement in the time left to you.

When to Start?

We've set up the schedule on the next page as a hypothetical week from Wednesday to Tuesday. Of course, you're free to start on any day you like. But, if at all possible, try to:

➤ START YOUR SAT-IN-A-WEEK PROGRAM

   AT LEAST TEN DAYS BEFORE THE EXAM

For instance, try to arrange your schedule so you complete the 15-step program on Tuesday or Wednesday for an SAT administered on Saturday.

➤ DO NO MORE THAN ONE DAY'S WORK IN A SINGLE DAY

You may be tempted to read through the book as quickly as possible, but don't. It's better to give yourself time to absorb what you're learning.

➤ TAKE A FULL-LENGTH PRACTICE TEST UNDER TIMED CONDITIONS

Choose an actual published SAT, or the tests contained in some of the other Kaplan SAT books listed below. Don't worry too much about your score on whatever practice test you take; that score doesn't count. Instead, try to get a feel for what it's like to take a long test under timed conditions. But please, don't take a full-length practice test less than 48 hours before your actual SAT! For one thing, you won't have time to use the results to assess your strengths and weaknesses and focus your last hours of study. And if you try to take two full tests in such close proximity, you'll just exhaust yourself. That does you more harm than good.

If you've got significantly more than ten days to study, of course, you should consider using a more comprehensive SAT prep book, such as Kaplan's *SAT: The Classic Course* or our separate *SAT Math* and *Verbal Workbooks*. A smaller book, *SAT Sneak Preview*, would be good to use as a full-length practice test. You might even sign up for a live SAT course if you have a month or more. You can call us at 1-800-KAP-TEST for further information.

But since you've read this far, it's likely that you don't have all that much time before your SAT. And it's for you that this book was designed. Use it wisely, and a week or two from now you'll walk into the SAT as you should walk into any test — confident and prepared.

                                                     How To Use This Book

Start your SAT-In-A-Week program at least ten days before the exam.

For instance, try to arrange your schedule so you complete the 15-step program on Tuesday or Wednesday for an SAT administered on Saturday.

Do no more than one day's work in a single day.

Take a full-length practice test under timed conditions.

Choose an actual published SAT, or the tests contained in some of the other Kaplan SAT books listed on the previous page. You can call us at 1-800-KAP-TEST.

Wednesday/Day 1	**Begin Study Program** Steps 1,2
Thursday/Day 2	**Study Program** Steps 3,4
Friday/Day 3	**Study Program** Steps 5,6,7
Saturday/Day 4	**Study Program** Steps 8,9
Sunday/Day 5	**Study Program** Steps 10,11
Monday/Day 6	**Study Program** Step 12
Tuesday/Day 7	**End Study Program** Steps 13,14,15
Wednesday	**Take Practice Test** *Use actual time limits!*
Thursday	**Review Practice Test** *Re-do steps in which you were weak.*
Friday	**Rest and Mental Prep** *Read over Recaps one last time.*
Saturday	**SAT Test! Good Luck!**

✔ At-a-Glance

Below are the topics covered in today's lesson. Check each topic as you complete it. If you ha time later, come back to any topics you've skipped not understood entirely.

STEP 1 — SAT KNOW-HOW

❏ Three Principles of SAT Know-How
❏ Using the Structure of the SAT to Your Advantage
❏ The Top Four General Question Strategi
(*Time: 30 minutes*)

STEP 2 — FORMAT ORIENTATION

❏ The Setup of the Test
❏ Analogies
❏ Sentence Completions
❏ Critical Reading
❏ Regular Math
❏ Quantitative Comparisons
❏ Grid-ins
(*Time: 30 minutes*)

Step 1: SAT Know-How

TESTING WELL IS THE BEST REVENGE

To perform well on the SAT, you naturally need some basic math and verbal skills. But you also need something else that the College Board doesn't mention — standardized-test smarts. You need to understand how the test works and how you can turn the test's structure to your own advantage. What you need is SAT know-how. Attaining that know-how, and the confidence it produces, is what this book is all about.

But can you gain this kind of know-how in a single week? Well, just remember that a little expertise can go a long way on the SAT. Getting just one extra question right every ten minutes translates to 15 more correct scored answers over the entire exam. This improvement could boost your scaled score by close to 150 points!

Remember, too, that you don't need to get 85% or 90% of the questions right on the SAT to get a good score. With little more than 75% of the questions correct you can get double 600s — a very solid performance (the Math and Verbal sections are each scored on a scale of 200 to 800). In fact, you can get four out of every ten questions wrong and still get twin 500s!

❏ THREE SIMPLE PRINCIPLES OF SAT KNOW-HOW

There are three simple things you need to master the SAT.

➤ You need to have a basic understanding of SAT content (Math and Verbal).

➤ You need to hone the thinking and testing skills that underlie the SAT.

➤ You need to gain familiarity with the unique nature of the SAT.

Content and skills are obviously important. You can't do well without them, and that's why we'll be covering them in the steps to come. But understanding the way the SAT works — its setup, its structure, and the traps it often lays for you — will allow you to gain points on the test that you might not otherwise have gotten. This is an area where a little prep can go a long way toward improving your score!

❑ USING THE STRUCTURE OF THE SAT TO YOUR ADVANTAGE

The SAT is different from the tests you're used to taking. On a school test, you probably go through the problems in order. You spend more time on hard questions than on easy ones, since this is where you get more points. And you often show your work, since the teacher tells you that how you approach a problem is as important as getting the answer right.

None of this works on the SAT. In SAT land, you *can* benefit from moving around within a section, the hard questions *aren't* worth more than the easy ones, and it *doesn't* matter how you answer the question — only what your answer is. What's more, time pressure is much more intense on the SAT than on your average high school exam.

To succeed on this unusual kind of test, you need to know some fundamentals about its overall structure.

THE SAT IS HIGHLY PREDICTABLE

Because the format and directions of the SAT remain unchanged from test to test, you can learn the setup in advance. On test day, Analogies, Quantitative Comparisons (QCs), and Grid-ins shouldn't be new to you. Neither should the setup of any other question type or section.

One of the easiest things you can do to help your performance on the SAT is to understand the directions before taking the test. Since the instructions are always exactly the same, there's no reason to waste your time on test day reading them.

Learn the directions before test day.

MOST SAT QUESTIONS ARE ARRANGED IN ORDER OF DIFFICULTY

Not all the questions on the SAT are equally difficult. Each test section is made up of one, two, or three different sets of questions. Except for the Critical Reading problems, the questions always get tougher as you work through an individual set.

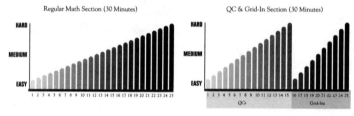

Questions get harder as you move through a set.

Here's how to use this pattern to your advantage: As you work, you should always be aware of where you are in the set. When working on the easy problems, you can generally trust your first impulse — the obvious answer is likely to be right.

As you get to the end of the set, you need to become more suspicious. Now the answers probably won't come easily — and if they do, be careful, because the obvious answer is likely to be wrong. Watch out for the answer that just "looks right." It may be a distractor — a wrong answer choice meant to entice you. It may, in other words, be a trap.

---❖---

**Trust your first impulse on early, easy questions;
think twice on late, difficult questions.**

---❖---

YOU NEEDN'T ANSWER THE QUESTIONS IN THE ORDER GIVEN

You're allowed to skip around within each section of the SAT. High scorers know this. They move through the test efficiently. They don't dwell on any one question, even a hard one, until they've tried every question at least once.

When you run into questions that look tough, circle them in your test booklet and skip them for the time being. (Make sure to skip them on your answer grid, too.) If you have time, go back and try again after you've answered the others. On a second look, these circled questions can turn out to be amazingly simple. (A general point: Don't be afraid to mark up your test book — not only to circle questions and choices, but to do math work, to underline important things in reading passages, etc.)

If you've started answering a question and get confused, quit and go on to the next question. Persistence may pay off in school, but it usually hurts your SAT score. Don't spend so much time answering one tough question that you use up three or four questions' worth of time. That can cost you points, even if you get the hard question right.

---❖---

**Skip questions that look too time-consuming.
Come back to them later if you have time.**

---❖---

THERE'S A GUESSING PENALTY THAT CAN ACTUALLY WORK IN YOUR FAVOR

The test makers like to talk about the guessing penalty on the SAT. But "guessing penalty" is a misnomer. It's really a wrong-answer penalty. If you guess wrong (except in Grid-ins), you get penalized. If you guess right, you get a point.

The fact is, if you can eliminate one or more choices as definitely wrong, you'll turn the odds in your favor and actually come out ahead by guessing.

Here's how the penalty works:

➤ If you get an answer wrong on a Quantitative Comparison, which has four answer choices, you lose 1/3 point.

➤ If you get an answer wrong on any other multiple-choice questions, which have five answer choices, you lose 1/4 point.

➤ If you get an answer wrong on a Grid-in Math question, where you write in your own answers, *you lose nothing*.

The fractional points you lose are meant to offset the points you might get "accidentally" by guessing the correct answer. With practice, though, it's often easy to eliminate several answer choices on many problems. By learning the techniques for eliminating wrong answer choices, you can actually turn the guessing "penalty" to your advantage.

—————— ❖ ——————

Guess if you can't answer the question, but can eliminate at least one choice.

—————— ❖ ——————

THE ANSWER GRID HAS NO HEART

It sounds simple but it's extremely important: Don't make mistakes filling out your answer grid! When time is short, it's easy to get confused going back and forth between your test book and your grid. If you know the answer, but misgrid, you won't get the points.

To avoid mistakes on the answer grid:

> ALWAYS CIRCLE THE QUESTIONS YOU SKIP

Put a big circle in your test book around the number of any question you skip. When you go back, such questions will be easy to locate. Also, if you accidentally skip a box on the grid, you can more easily check your grid against your book to see where you went wrong.

In the test book, circle the questions you skip .

> ALWAYS CIRCLE THE ANSWERS YOU CHOOSE

Circling your answers in the test book also makes it easier to check your grid against your book.

In the test book, circle the answers you choose.

> GRID FIVE OR MORE ANSWERS AT ONCE

Don't transfer your answers to the grid after every question. Transfer your answers after every five questions, or at the end of each reading passage. (When time is running out at the end of a section, though, start gridding one by one — so you don't get caught at the end with ungridded answers!) That way, you won't keep breaking your concentration to mark the grid. You'll save time and improve accuracy.

Grid answers in groups of five or more.

❑ THE TOP FOUR GENERAL QUESTION STRATEGIES

Apart from knowing the setup of the SAT, you've got to have a system for attacking the questions. Now that you know some basics about how the test is set up, you can approach each section with a bit more strategy in mind. What follows is the best method for approaching SAT questions systematically. (We'll talk about specific question strategies — those that take advantage of the structural peculiarities of each particular question type — in later steps throughout this book.)

1. THINK ABOUT THE QUESTION BEFORE YOU LOOK AT THE ANSWER

The people who make the test love to put distractors among the answer choices. Distractors are answer choices that look like the right answer, but aren't. If you jump right into the answer choices without thinking first about what you're looking for, you're much more likely to fall for one of these traps. In most cases, you're better off knowing what you're shopping for before you enter the store. The SAT is no different.

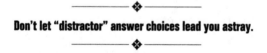

Don't let "distractor" answer choices lead you astray.

2. ELIMINATE ANY CHOICES YOU CAN BEFORE GUESSING

You already know that the "guessing penalty" can work in your favor. Don't just skip questions you can't answer. Spend some time with them to see if you can eliminate any of the answer choices. If you can eliminate any that are obviously bad, you should guess; with each choice you eliminate, you'll improve your chances of getting the question right.

❖

Eliminate bad choices to improve your guessing average.

❖

---

3. PACE YOURSELF

The SAT gives you a lot of questions in a short period of time. To get through a whole section, you can't spend too much time on any one question. Keep moving through the test at a good speed; if you run into a hard question, circle it in your test booklet, skip it, and come back to it later if you have time.

In the box below is a list of recommended average times per question. This doesn't mean that you should spend exactly 40 seconds on every Analogy. It's just a guide. Remember, the questions get harder as you move through a problem set. Ideally, you can work through the easy problems at a brisk, steady clip, and use a little more of your time for the harder ones that come at the end of the set. One caution: Don't completely rush through the easy problems just to save time for the harder ones. These early problems are points in your pocket, and you're better off not getting to the last couple of problems rather than carelessly missing these easy points.

RECOMMENDED TIMING

Section	On Average
Analogies	40 Seconds
Sentence Completions	40 Seconds
Critical Reading*	75 Seconds
Regular Math	70 Seconds
QCs	45 Seconds
Grid-Ins	90 Seconds

* Average time for Critical Reading includes time to read the passage. Spend about 30 seconds per question.

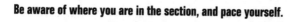

Be aware of where you are in the section, and pace yourself.

---

4. LOCATE QUICK POINTS IF YOU'RE RUNNING OUT OF TIME

Some questions can be done quickly; for instance, some reading questions will ask you to identify the meaning of a particular word in the passage. These can be done at the last minute, even if you haven't read the passage. On most Quantitative Comparisons, even the hardest ones, you can quickly eliminate at least one answer, improving your chances of guessing correctly. When you start to run out of time, locate and answer any of the quick points that remain. Don't panic. Many people who don't finish the SAT still get top scores.

When time is short, focus on the easy points.

Just remember that when you take the SAT, you have one clear objective in mind: to score as many points as you can. It's that simple. The rest of this book will help you do it — in the shortest time possible.

The Important Tips From This Step

➤ Learn the directions before test day.

➤ Trust your first impulse on early, easy questions; think twice on late, difficult questions.

➤ Skip questions that look too time-consuming. Come back to them later if you have time.

➤ Guess if you can't answer the question, but can eliminate at least one choice.

➤ In the test book, circle the questions you skip.

➤ In the test book, circle the answers you choose.

➤ Grid answers in groups of five or more.

➤ Don't let "distractor" answer choices lead you astray.

➤ Eliminate bad choices to improve your guessing average.

➤ Be aware of where you are in the section, and pace yourself.

➤ When time is short, focus on the easy points.

Step 2: Format Orientation

IT PAYS TO KNOW THE LAY OF THE LAND

Now that you've got some basic test-taking know-how under your belt, it's important to look more closely at the exact format of the test. When you sit down to take the SAT, you should already know what kinds of questions you'll find, what the instructions say, how the test will be scored, and how you will be timed.

Before we say anything else, though, we want to assure you that, no matter what you may have heard, the SAT is a skills test, not an IQ test. In fact, the test makers have now formally acknowledged this fact by changing the name of the test. Before 1994, "SAT" stood for Scholastic Aptitude Test; now it stands for Scholastic Assessment Test.

In other words, even the test makers now admit that you can improve your SAT score by developing your academic skills.

❏ THE SETUP OF THE TEST

There are six types of questions on the SAT: three verbal and three math. The likely number of questions you'll see of each type is listed below.

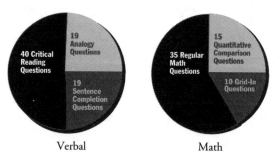

Verbal   Math

Verbal
> ➤ 19 Analogies
> ➤ 19 Sentence Completions
> ➤ 40 Critical Reading questions

Math
> ➤ 15 Quantitative Comparisons
> ➤ 35 Regular Math questions
> ➤ 10 Grid-ins

We'll talk in more detail about these questions below.

SECTION BREAKDOWN

The SAT is divided into seven sections, which can appear in any order.

> ➤ two 30-minute Verbal sections with Analogies, Sentence Completions, and Critical Reading
> ➤ one 15-minute Verbal section with Critical Reading
> ➤ one 30-minute section with QCs and Grid-ins
> ➤ one 30-minute section with Regular Math
> ➤ one 15-minute section with Regular Math
> ➤ one 30-minute experimental section (either Math or Verbal)

Don't fret about the so-called experimental section. This section, which is used to try out new questions, doesn't affect your score. It can show up any place and it will look like any other Verbal or Math section. Don't try to figure out which section is Experimental, and don't plan to nap during that period. First of all, you'll lose your momentum in the middle of the test. Second — and more important — you might be wrong.

❖

**Don't try to guess which section is experimental.
Try your best on all sections.**

❖

SCORING

You get 1 point for each correct answer on the SAT, and lose a fraction of a point for each wrong answer (except for Grid-ins, where you lose nothing for a wrong answer). If you leave a question blank, nothing happens to your score. The totals for the 78 Verbal and 60 Math scored questions are added up, and that produces two raw scores.

These numbers aren't your SAT scores. The raw scores are converted into scaled scores, each on a scale of 200 to 800; these are the scores that are reported to you and the colleges you choose.

SAT PARTICULARS

The SAT:

> ➤ is three hours long
> ➤ includes two 10-minute breaks (after sections 2 and 4)

There are some rules about how you may and may not allocate this time:

> ➤ You *may* move around within a section.
> ➤ You *may* flip through your section at the beginning to see what type of questions you have to answer.
> ➤ You *may not* jump back and forth between sections.
> ➤ You *may not* return to earlier sections to change answers.
> ➤ You *may not* spend more than the allotted time on any section.

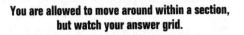

You are allowed to move around within a section,
but watch your answer grid.

❑ THE SETUP OF THE TEST: A CLOSER VIEW

Now that you have some idea of the general layout of the Math and
Verbal Sections of the SAT, let's take a closer look at the specific
question types you'll encounter:

THE VERBAL SECTIONS

✔ Analogies
✔ Sentence Completions
✔ Critical Reading

Analogies (19 questions): test your vocabulary and your understanding of word relationships.

You will see a pair of words in capital letters that are related in
some way. These are called the stem words. There will also be five
answer choices, each consisting of a word pair. For example:

> SNAKE:SLITHER::
> (A) egg:hatch
> (B) wolf:howl
> (C) rabbit:hop
> (D) turtle:snap
> (E) tarantula:bite

Your task is to identify the word pair that is related in the same
way as the stem words.

To succeed, THINK carefully about the stem words and establish the relationship in your mind before looking at the answer choices. It helps to "build a bridge" — to relate the two words in a sentence in a meaningful way.

The answer: C. To see how it's done, see Step 6, page 58.

❖

Think carefully about the stem before rushing to the choices.

❖

Sentence Completions (19 questions): test your vocabulary and your understanding of the structure and logic of sentences.

You will see a sentence with one or two blanks, plus five answer choices. For example:

> One striking aspect of Caribbean music is its——— of many African musical ———, such as call-and-response singing and polyrhythms.
>
> (A) recruitment..groups
>
> (B) proficiency..events
>
> (C) expectation..ideas
>
> (D) absorption..forms
>
> (E) condescension..priorities

Your task is to select the word or words that satisfactorily complete the sentence.

To succeed, THINK carefully about the sentence, looking for hidden definitions, structural signals, and other clues. Then predict an answer before looking at the answer choices.

The answer: D. To see how it's done, see Step 9, page 103.

❖

Look for hidden definitions, structural signals, and other clues.

❖

Critical Reading (40 questions): tests your ability to understand the content of written material, both fiction and nonfiction. Some questions also test your understanding of Vocabulary-in-Context. Reading questions account for more than half the Verbal questions on the SAT.

You will see four passages, of 400 to 850 words each, followed by multiple-choice questions. One of the passages will consist of a pair of related excerpts (this double passage will have questions that ask you to compare the two passages). Here's a shortened example:

> *The following is an excerpt from an article in a literary journal:*
>
> No doubt because it painted a less than flattering picture of life in America for Asian immigrants, *East Goes West* was not well received by contemporary literary critics. According to them, Kang's book displayed a curious lack of insight regarding the American effort to accommodate those who had come over from Korea. The facet of the novel reviewers did find praiseworthy was Han's perseverance and sustained optimism in the face of adversity.
>
> The passage indicates that the response of critics to *East Goes West* was one of
>
> (A) irony regarding the difference between Han's expectations and reality
>
> (B) admiration of the courage and creativity Kang showed in breaking from literary tradition
>
> (C) qualified disapproval of Kang's perception of his adopted homeland
>
> (D) confusion about the motivation of the protagonist
>
> (E) anger that Kang had so viciously attacked American society

Your task is to answer questions about the main ideas, details, inferences, arguments, and tone of the reading passages.

To succeed, read actively, not passively. THINK every step of the way about what the passage conveys, why the author uses a particular prose style, and what he or she is suggesting between the lines.

The answer: C. To see how it's done, see Steps 10 and 11, pages 118 and 130.

———————— ❖ ————————

Read actively, not passively.

———————— ❖ ————————

THE MATH SECTIONS

✔ Regular Math

✔ Quantitative Comparisons

✔ Grid-ins

(You can use a calculator on the SAT. In Step 7 we'll show you how to determine when a calculator can help you and when it can actually hurt.)

Regular Math (35 questions): tests your ability to do standard math questions.

You will see problems in arithmetic, algebra, and geometry, with multiple-choice answers. For example:

> At the Frosty Ice Cream store, the number of cones sold fell by 20 percent in November. If sales fell by a further 25 percent in December, what was the percent decrease in the number of cones sold in the whole two-month period?
>
> (A)   10%
>
> (B)   20%
>
> (C)   35%
>
> (D)   40%
>
> (E)   45%

Your task is to solve the problem quickly and spot the answer among five possible choices.

To succeed, THINK resourcefully, working from the given information to the desired answer. Look for patterns, shortcuts, and traps (like the one lurking in this question, which might lead you to blindly add and subtract percentages).

The answer: D. To see how it's done, see Step 3 (page 24), Step 8 (page 84), and Step 12 (page 146).

Look for patterns, shortcuts, and traps.

Quantitative Comparisons (QCs) (15 questions): test your ability to examine sets of numbers and to determine relationships.

You will see two quantities, one in Column A and one in Column B. For example:

Column A	Column B
$\sqrt{5} + \sqrt{5}$	$\sqrt{10}$

Your task is to decide if one quantity is greater than the other; if the two quantities are equal; or if you don't have enough information to decide.

To succeed, compare without calculating. THINK quickly about the quantities, then look for a fast and clever way to decide which is bigger.

The answer: A. To see how it's done, see Step 4, page 32.

Compare, don't calculate, on QCs.

Grid-ins (10 questions): test your ability to figure out your own answers to math problems. They are called "Grid-ins" because you have to fill in your answer on a special grid; there are no multiple-choice answers. Grid-ins account for 10 of the 60 math questions.

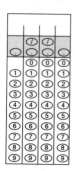

You will see the same kinds of problems as Regular Math, but the right answer won't be on the page in front of you.

Your task is to figure out the problem and fill in your answer on a grid.

To succeed, practice doing Grid-in problems to get comfortable with the procedure. Remember, if you mis grid an answer, you can lose the point, even if you did all the right math. Often there is more than one correct way to fill in a grid; sometimes there is a whole range of correct answers. As always, though, THINK your way through the problems first.

The answer: Let's say your answer to a Grid-in problem is $4\frac{1}{2}$. Part of the task with Grid-ins is indicating the correct answer correctly on your answer grid. To see how it's done, see Step 13, page 175.

———————— ❖ ————————

Practice gridding in until it comes as second nature.

———————— ❖ ————————

Step 2 Recap: Format Orientation

The Important Tips From This Step

➤ Don't try to guess which section is experimental. Try your best on all sections.

➤ You are allowed to move around within a section, but watch your answer grid.

➤ Think carefully about the question stem before rushing to the choices.

➤ Look for hidden definitions, structural signals, and other clues.

➤ Read actively, not passively.

➤ Look for patterns, shortcuts, and traps.

➤ Compare, don't calculate, on QCs.

➤ Practice gridding in until it comes as second nature.

Demystifying SAT Math

THE STEPS

✔ At-a-Glance

Below are the topics covered in today's lesson. Check each topic as you complete it. If you have time later, come back to any topics you've skipped or not understood entirely.

STEP 3 — BASIC MATH STRATEGIES

❑ How SAT Math Is Set Up
❑ The Math Directions
❑ How to Approach SAT Math
(*Time: 30 minutes*)

STEP 4 — QC TECHNIQUES

❑ The Format
❑ Two Rules for Choice (D)
❑ Kaplan's Top Four QC Strategies
(*Time: 60 minutes*)

Step 3: Basic Math Strategies

SAT MATH DOES NOT EQUAL THE SUM OF ALL MATHEMATICS

The term "mathematics" covers many things — linear algebra and complex analysis, topology and trigonometry, number theory and multivariable calculus. Mathematics is a huge and daunting field, requiring years of study to master.

But SAT Math is different. To ace the SAT, you need only a small body of mathematical knowledge, covering basic concepts in arithmetic, algebra, and geometry. In this book, we'll cover most of what you need to know. But remember: Just as important as knowing the mathematical concepts is understanding the ways in which they are tested on the SAT— knowing the twists and turns the test makers throw into many Math problems.

❑ HOW SAT MATH IS SET UP

There are three scored Math sections on the new SAT:
- ➤ one 30-minute section with 25 Regular Math questions
- ➤ one 30-minute section with a set of 15 QCs and a set of ten Grid-ins
- ➤ one 15-minute section with 10 Regular Math questions

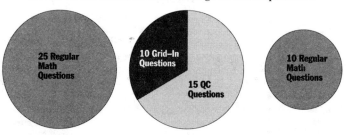

25 Regular Math Questions

10 Grid–In Questions

15 QC Questions

10 Regular Math Questions

DIFFICULTY LEVEL

All sets of SAT Math questions start off easy and gradually increase in difficulty.

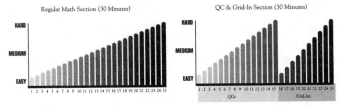

Regular Math Section (30 Minutes)   QC & Grid-In Section (30 Minutes)

Always be aware of the difficulty level as you go through a question set. Easy problems call for different approaches. The harder the question, the more traps you'll encounter. If you know you're dealing with a hard question (even though it may look easy), you'll be prepared.

❑ THE MATH DIRECTIONS

You'll save a lot of time on SAT Math by knowing the directions in advance. They take a long time to plow through, and they are the same for every test. After reading this book, you'll know what to do with each question type, so you can skip the directions and go straight to the first question.

At the start of each Math section you will find the following information:

Time—30 Minutes 25 Questions	Solve each of the following problems, decide which is the best answer choice, and darken the corresponding oval on the answer sheet. Use available space in the test booklet for scratchwork.

Notes:

(1) Calculator use is permitted.

(2) All numbers used are real numbers.

(3) Figures are provided for some problems. All figures are drawn to scale and lie in a plane UNLESS otherwise indicated.

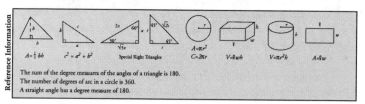

Reference Information

$A = \frac{1}{2}bh$　　$c^2 = a^2 + b^2$　　Special Right Triangles　　$A = \pi r^2$　　$C = 2\pi r$　　$V = \ell wh$　　$V = \pi r^2 h$　　$A = \ell w$

The sum of the degree measures of the angles of a triangle is 180.
The number of degrees of arc in a circle is 360.
A straight angle has a degree measure of 180.

➤ Note (2) means you won't have to deal with imaginary numbers, like i (the square root of -1).

➤ Note (3) tells you diagrams are drawn to scale (unless otherwise noted), which means you can use these diagrams to estimate measurements. However, if a diagram is labeled "Figure not drawn to scale," you can't do this.

➤ Note (3)'s reference to figures that "lie in a plane" simply means that you are dealing with flat figures, like rectangles or circles, unless the question says otherwise.

➤ The math information you're given includes many basic geometry formulas. By test day you should know all of these formulas. But if you find yourself drawing a blank on test day, it's nice to know that the formulas are spelled out in the directions.

➤ The QCs and Grid-ins have different instructions, which we'll discuss in detail later.

❖

**Learn the math directions now so that you don't even
have to look at them on test day.**

❖

❏ HOW TO APPROACH SAT MATH

To maximize your Math score, you need to use your time efficiently.
Then you won't get bogged down on a single hard question and miss
other problems you could have solved if you'd had more time.

The key to working systematically is to *think about the question
before you look for the answer*. A few seconds spent up front looking for
traps, thinking about your approach, and deciding whether to tackle
the problem now or come back to it later will pay off in SAT points.
On easy problems, you may know what to do right away. But on hard
problems, the few extra seconds are time well spent.

THE KAPLAN SYSTEMATIC APPROACH TO MATH QUESTIONS

Let's see how you might use a systematic approach to the problem
below:

12. At a certain diner, Joe orders 3 donuts and a cup of coffee
    and is charged $2.25. Stella orders 2 donuts and a cup of
    coffee and is charged $1.70. What is the price of 2 donuts?
    (A) $0.55
    (B) $0.60
    (C) $1.10
    (D) $1.30
    (E) $1.80

STEP 1: ASSESS THE QUESTION'S DIFFICULTY

All SAT Math questions are arranged in order of difficulty. Within a set, the first questions are easy, the middle ones moderately difficult, and the last ones are hard. Problem #12 above should be a moderately difficult word problem.

STEP 2: READ THROUGH THE QUESTION CAREFULLY

If you try to start solving the problem before reading it all the way through, you may end up doing unnecessary work.

> HINT: On difficult questions, watch out for Math Traps. Hard questions are often designed to trip up careless readers. (For more on Math Traps, see Step 12.)

Make sure you know what's being asked. Problem #12 looks straightforward, but read through it carefully and you'll see a slight twist. You're asked to find the cost of *two* donuts, not one. Many people will find the price of a single donut and forget to double it. That's why this problem is #12 and not #2: There's a twist to it.

STEP 3: DECIDE WHETHER TO DO THE PROBLEM OR SKIP IT FOR NOW

If you have *no* idea what to do, skip the problem. Spend your time on the problems you can solve.

If you think you can solve it, but it will take a lot of time, circle the question number in your test booklet and make a note to come back to it later if you have time.

If you can eliminate one or more answer choices, do so. Make an educated guess. In your test booklet, make a note to remind yourself that you guessed, and try solving the problem later if time permits. (For details on educated guessing, see Step 14.)

STEP 4: IF YOU DO TACKLE THE PROBLEM, LOOK FOR THE FASTEST APPROACH

Look for hidden information. On an easy question all the information you need to solve the problem may be given up front, in the stem, or in a diagram. But in a harder question, you may need to look for hidden information. Also, extraneous information may be thrown into the problem to get you off track. Since questions are arranged in order of difficulty, you should be a little wary of #12. If you got the answer too easily, you may have missed something. In this case, you're asked to find the price of two donuts, not one.

❖

Make sure you know exactly what is being asked.

❖

Look for shortcuts. Sometimes the obvious way of doing a problem is the long way. If the method you choose involves lots of calculating, look for another route. There's usually more than one way to solve a problem, and one of those ways won't involve you in tons of arithmetic. In problem #12, for example, the cost of donuts and coffee could be translated into two distinct equations using the variables d (for "donut") and c (for "coffee"). You could find c in terms of d, then plug this in to the other equation. But if you think carefully, you'll see there's a quicker way: The difference in price between 3 donuts and a cup of coffee and 2 donuts and a cup of coffee is the price of 1 donut. So one donut costs $2.25 - $1.70 = $0.55. (Remember, you have to find the price of 2 donuts. Twice $0.55 is $1.10.)

❖

Look for shortcuts.

❖

Use a variety of strategies. The Math chapters of this book will review many strategies for specific problem types that will help you get to the answer faster.

STEP 5: IF YOU GET STUCK, MAKE AN EDUCATED GUESS

If you're not sure what to do, or if you've tried solving a problem but got stuck, cut your losses. Eliminate whatever choices you can, and then guess. Since the Math choices are typically arranged in increasing or decreasing order, it's often easy to find and eliminate choices that are way too high or low.

> HINT: When you skip a question, circle it or make a note in your test booklet to come back to it later, if you have time.

Let's say it's taking too long to solve the donut problem. Can you eliminate any answer choices? The price of two donuts and a cup of coffee is $1.70. That means the cost of two donuts alone can't be $1.80, which eliminates choice (E). Now you can choose between the remaining choices, and your odds of guessing correctly have improved.

If you get stuck, make an educated guess.

If you practice using this 5-Step Systematic Approach to the Math problems on the SAT, you will save time and avoid mistakes on test day.

Use the Kaplan Systematic Approach to Math questions.

Step 3 Recap: Basic Math Strategies

The Important Tips From This Step

➤ Learn the Math directions now so that you don't even have to look at them on test day.

➤ Make sure you know exactly what is being asked.

➤ Look for shortcuts.

➤ If you get stuck, make an educated guess.

➤ Use the Kaplan 5-Step Systematic Approach to Math Questions:

  1. Assess Difficulty
  2. Read Question Carefully
  3. Decide to Do or Skip
  4. Look for Fastest Approach
  5. If Stuck, Make an Educated Guess

Step 4: QC Techniques

QCS ARE A GIFT TO THOSE IN THE KNOW

In Quantitative Comparisons, instead of solving for a particular value, you need to compare two quantities. At first, QCs may appear really difficult because of their unfamiliar format. However, once you get used to them, they can be quicker and easier than the other types of Math questions, and a surefire way to pile up fast points.

STATISTIC: The 15 QCs count for one-fourth of your Math score.

❏ The Format

WHERE THEY APPEAR

The 15 QCs appear in the 30-minute Math section that also contains the ten Grid-in questions (you'll learn about those in Step 13). The QCs are arranged in order of increasing difficulty.

THE DIRECTIONS

The directions you'll see will look something like those below. Don't freak! We'll explain them in real English.

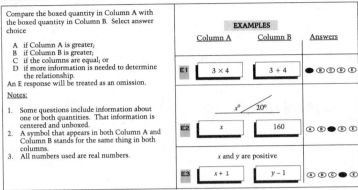

❖

Memorize what the QC answer choices stand for. Know them cold by test day.

❖

As you've seen, the above directions can be intimidating. What they boil down to is this: In each question, you'll see two mathematical expressions, one in Column A, the other in Column B. Here's a sample:

Column A	Column B
$x(x - 1)$	$x^2 - x$

Some questions include additional information about one or both quantities. This information will be centered above the two quantities.

Your job is to compare the quantities in each column. If Column A is bigger, choose (A); if Column B is bigger, choose (B); if they're equal, choose (C); and if you don't have enough information to tell, choose (D).

Warning: Choice (E) is never the answer to a QC. Be careful not to mark (E) when you mean (D).

❖

Never mark choice (E) on a QC.

❖

❏ TWO RULES FOR ANSWER CHOICE (D)

Notice that choices (A), (B), and (C) all represent definite relationships between the quantities in Column A and Column B. But choice (D) represents a relationship that cannot be determined. Here are two things to remember about choice (D) that will help you decide when to pick it:

1. CHOICE (D) IS NEVER CORRECT IF BOTH COLUMNS CONTAIN ONLY NUMBERS, WITHOUT VARIABLES.

The relationship between numbers is unchanging and can always be established, but choice (D) means that more than one relationship is possible.

❖

Never pick choice (D) if both columns in a QC contain only numbers (no variables).

❖
---

2. CHOICE (D) IS CORRECT IF YOU CAN DEMONSTRATE TWO DIFFERENT RELATIONSHIPS BETWEEN THE COLUMNS.

Suppose you ran across the following QC:

Column A	Column B
2x	3x

If x is a positive number, Column B is greater than Column A. If $x = 0$, the columns are equal. If x equals any negative number, Column B is less than Column A. Since more than one relationship is possible, (D) must be correct. In fact, as soon as you find a second possibility, stop work and pick choice (D).

❖

**If you can demonstrate two *different* relationships
between the columns, pick choice (D).**

❖

☐ COMPARE, DON'T CALCULATE: KAPLAN'S TOP FOUR STRATEGIES FOR QCs

The key to QC success is not spending time on elaborate calculations. Remember that you're not looking for a specific answer here; you're just looking for the relative size of the two quantities. So, instead of calculating, *compare* the two quantities.

Here are four top Kaplan strategies that will enable you to make quick comparisons.

STRATEGY 1: MAKE ONE COLUMN LOOK LIKE THE OTHER

When the quantities in Columns A and B are expressed differently, you can often make the comparison easier by changing one column to look like the other. For example, if one column is a percent, and the other a fraction, try converting the fraction to a percent. Or, if the expression under Column A is in hours while that under Column B is in minutes, put the two on an equal footing by converting the figure in Column A to minutes.

Column A	Column B
$x(x - 1)$	$x^2 - x$

Here Column A has parentheses, and Column B doesn't. So make Column A look more like Column B: Get rid of those parentheses. You end up with $x^2 - x$ in both columns, which means they are equal and the answer is (C).

Try another example, this one involving geometry.

Column A	Column B

The diameter of circle O is d and the area is a.

Column A	Column B
$\frac{\pi d^2}{2}$	a

Make Column B look more like Column A by rewriting a, the area of the circle, in terms of the diameter, d. The area of any circle equals πr^2, where r is the radius.

Since the radius is half the diameter, we can plug in $\frac{d}{2}$ for r in the area formula to get $\pi(\frac{d}{2})^2$ in Column B. Simplifying, we get $\frac{\pi d^2}{4}$. Since both columns now contain πd^2 in the numerator, we can get rid of both and simply compare $\frac{1}{2}$ with $\frac{1}{4}$. Column A is greater, so the answer is choice (A).

——————— ❖ ———————

Make the terms in both columns similar.

——————— ❖ ———————

STRATEGY 2: DO THE SAME THING TO BOTH COLUMNS

Some QC questions become much clearer if you change not just the appearances, but the values of both columns. Treat them like two sides of an inequality, with the sign temporarily hidden.

You can add or subtract the same amount from both columns, and multiply or divide by the same *positive* amount without altering the relationship.

But watch out. Multiplying or dividing an inequality by a negative number reverses the direction of the inequality sign, as does squaring a fraction, so don't do it.

> WARNING: Don't multiply or divide both QC columns by a negative number. Be careful with fractions. Remember that negative numbers and fractions behave very differently from positive integers!

In the QC below, what could you do to both columns?

Column A		Column B
	$4a + 3 = 7b$	
$20a + 10$		$35b - 5$

All the terms in the two columns are multiples of 5, so divide both columns by 5 to simplify. You're left with $4a + 2$ in Column A and $7b - 1$ in Column B. This resembles the equation given in the centered information. In fact, if you add 1 to both columns, you have $4a + 3$ in Column A and $7b$ in Column B. The centered equation tells us they are equal. Thus choice (C) is correct.

In the next QC, what could you do to both columns?

Column A		Column B
	$y > 0$	
$1 + \frac{y}{(1+y)}$		$1 + \frac{1}{(1+y)}$

Solution: First subtract 1 from both sides. That gives you $\frac{y}{(1+y)}$ in Column A, and $\frac{1}{(1+y)}$ in Column B. Get rid of the identical denominators and you're left comparing y with 1.

You know y is greater than 0, but it could be a fraction less than 1, so it could be greater or less than 1. Since you can't say for sure which column is greater, the answer is (D).

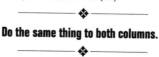

Do the same thing to both columns.

STRATEGY 3: PICK NUMBERS

If a QC involves variables, try picking numbers to make the relationship clearer. Here's what you do:

➤ Pick numbers that are easy to work with.

➤ Plug in the numbers and calculate the values. Note the relationship between the columns.

➤ Pick another number for each variable and calculate the values again. Is it the same relationship?

Column A		Column B
	$r > s > t > w > 0$	
$\frac{r}{t}$		$\frac{s}{w}$

Try $r = 4$, $s = 3$, $t = 2$, and $w = 1$. Then Column A $= \frac{r}{t} = \frac{4}{2} = 2$. And Column B $= \frac{s}{w} = \frac{3}{1} = 3$. So in this case Column B is greater than Column A.

Always Pick More Than One Number and Calculate Again

In the example above, we first found that Column B was bigger. But this doesn't mean that Column B is *always* bigger and that the answer is (B). It *does* mean that the answer is not (A) or (C). But the answer could still be (D), not enough information to decide.

If time is short here, guess between (B) and (D). But whenever you can, pick another set of numbers and calculate again.

Make a special effort to find a second set of numbers that will alter the relationship. Here for example, try making r a lot larger. Pick $r = 30$ and keep the other variables as they were. Now Column A = $\frac{30}{2} = 15$. This time, Column A is greater than Column B, so choice (D) is the correct answer.

IMPORTANT: *If the relationship between Columns A and B changes when you pick other numbers, (D) must be the answer.*

Pick Different Kinds of Numbers

Don't assume that all variables represent positive integers. Unless you're told otherwise, variables can represent zero, negative numbers, or fractions. Since different kinds of numbers behave differently, always pick a different kind of number the second time around. In the example above, we plugged in a small positive number the first time and a larger number the second.

In the next three examples, we pick different numbers in the way outlined above. In which cases is the answer (D)?

Column A	Column B
w	$-w$

If $w = 5$, Column A = 5 and Column B = -5, so Column A is greater.

If $w = -5$, Column A = -5 and Column B = 5, so Column B is greater.

We get a different relationship between the columns, so the answer is (D).

Column A	Column B
	$w \neq 0$
w	$\frac{1}{w}$

If w = 3, Column A = 3 and Column B = $\frac{1}{3}$, so Column A is greater.

If w = $\frac{1}{3}$, Column A = $\frac{1}{3}$ and Column B = $\frac{1}{\frac{1}{3}}$ = 3, so Column B is greater. Again, since the relationship changes depending on which numbers we pick, the answer is (D).

Column A		Column B
	$w > 1$	
w		w^2

If w = 1.1 , Column A = 1.1 and Column B = 1.21, so Column B is greater.

If w = 70, Column A = 70 and Column B = 4,900, so Column B is greater again. Here, we have not been able to demonstrate a changing relationship. The answer is B.

❖

**Plug in two different sets of numbers,
and compare columns for each.**

❖

STRATEGY 4: AVOID COMMON QC TRAPS

To avoid QC traps, always be alert. Don't assume anything. Be especially cautious near the end of the question set.

Don't be tricked by misleading information.

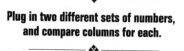

Column A	Column B
	John is taller than Bob.
John's weight in pounds	Bob's weight in pounds

The test makers hope you'll think, "If John is taller, he must weigh more." But there's no guaranteed relationship between height and weight, so you don't have enough information. The answer is (D).

Don't Assume

A common QC mistake is to assume that variables represent positive integers. As we saw in using the number-picking strategy, fractions or negative numbers often show another relationship between the columns.

<u>Column A</u>   <u>Column B</u>
When 1 is added to the square of x the result is 37.

x 6

It is easy to assume that x must be 6, since the square of x is 36. That would make choice (C) correct. However, it's possible that $x = -6$. Since x could be either 6 or -6, the answer is (D).

HINT: *Be aware of negative numbers!*

Don't Forget to Consider Other Possibilities

<u>Column A</u>   <u>Column B</u>

$$R$$
$$S$$
$$T$$
$$\overline{}$$
$$1W$$

In the addition problem above, R, S, and T are different digits that are multiples of 3, and W is a digit.

W 8

Since you're told that R, S, and T are digits and different multiples of 3, most people will think of 3, 6, and 9, which add up to 18. That makes W equal to 8, and Columns A and B equal. But that's too obvious for a QC at the end of the section.

There's another possibility: 0 is also a digit and a multiple of 3. So the three digits could be 0, 3, and 9, or 0, 6, and 9, which give totals of 12 and 15, respectively. That means W could be 8, 2, or 5. Since the columns could be equal, or Column B could be greater, answer choice (D) must be correct.

Don't Fall for Look-alikes

Column A	Column B
$\sqrt{5} + \sqrt{5}$	$\sqrt{10}$

At first glance, forgetting the rules of radicals, you might think that these quantities are equal and the answer is (C). But use some common sense to see this isn't the case. $\sqrt{5}$ has to be bigger than $\sqrt{4}$ (which is 2), so the $\sqrt{5} + \sqrt{5}$ in Column A has to be bigger than 4. The $\sqrt{10}$ in Column B, meanwhile, is *smaller* than another familiar number, $\sqrt{16}$, so Column B is less than 4. The answer is (A).

❖

Don't assume that all variables are positive numbers, or that numbers that look alike, are alike.

❖

Now that you've got a handle on QCs, finish off today's lesson with the following Pop Quiz:

7 questions
6 minutes

Column A		Column B

$x = 2y$
$y > 0$

1. 4^{2y} $\qquad\qquad\qquad$ 2^x

---

q, r, and s are positive integers
$qrs > 12$

2. $\frac{qr}{5}$ $\qquad\qquad\qquad$ $\frac{3}{s}$

$\frac{x}{y} = \frac{z}{4}$

x, y, and z are positive

3. $6x$ $\qquad\qquad\qquad$ $2yz$

$x > 1$
$y > 0$

4. y^x $\qquad\qquad\qquad$ $y^{(x+1)}$

$h > 1$

5. The number of minutes $\qquad\qquad$ $\frac{60}{h}$
   in h hours

$7p + 3 = r$
$3p + 7 = s$

6. r $\qquad\qquad\qquad$ s

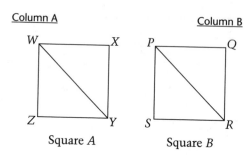

Column A

Column B

W ─── X   P ─── Q

Z ─── Y   S ─── R

Square *A*   Square *B*

Figures not drawn to scale.

7. $\dfrac{\text{Perimeter of square } A}{\text{Perimeter of square } B}$ $\dfrac{\text{Length of } WY}{\text{Length of } PR}$

EXPLANATIONS

1. (A)
Replacing the x exponent in Column B with the equivalent value given in the problem, we're comparing 4^{2y} to 2^{2y}. Since $y > 0$, raising 4 to the 2y power will result in a greater value than raising 2 to the 2y power.

2. (D)
Do the same thing to both columns to make them look like the centered information. When we multiply both sides by 5s we get qrs in Column A and 15 in Column B. Since qrs could be any integer greater than 12, it could be greater than, equal to, or less than 15.

3. (B)
Do the same thing to both columns until they resemble the centered information. When we divide both columns by 6y we get $\frac{6x}{6y}$, or $\frac{x}{y}$ in Column A, and $\frac{2yz}{6y}$, or $\frac{z}{3}$ in Column B. Since $\frac{x}{y} = \frac{z}{4}$, and $\frac{z}{3} > \frac{z}{4}$ (because z is positive), $\frac{z}{3} > \frac{x}{y}$.

4. (D)
Pick numbers. Try $x = y = 2$. Then Column A $= y^x = 2^2 = 4$. Column B $= y^x+1 = 2^3 = 8$, making Column B greater. But if $x = 2$ and $y = \frac{1}{2}$, Column A $= (\frac{1}{2})^2 = \frac{1}{4}$ and Column B $= (\frac{1}{2})^3 = \frac{1}{8}$. In this case, Column A is greater than Column B, so the answer is (D).

5. (A)
It's a trap! The "obvious" answer here is choice (C), because there are 60 minutes in an hour, and 60 appears in Column B. But the number of minutes in h hours would equal 60 times h, not 60 divided by h. Try picking numbers: If h is 2 (it has to be greater than 1), the number in

Column A would be 60(2) or 120. The number in Column B would be $\frac{60}{2}$, or 30. Column A is greater, and that holds even if you pick a much larger number for h. (A) is correct.

6. (D)
Pick a value for p, and see what effect this has on r and s. If $p = 1$, $r = (7 \times 1) + 3 = 10$, and $s = (3 \times 1) + 7 = 10$, and the two columns are equal. But if $p = 0$, $r = (7 \times 0) + 3 = 3$, and $s = (3 \times 0) + 7 = 7$, and Column A is smaller than Column B. Since there are at least two different possible relationships, the answer is choice (D).

7. (C)
We don't know the exact relationship between Square A and Square B, but it doesn't matter. The problem is actually just comparing the ratios of corresponding parts of two squares. Whatever the relationship between them is for one specific length in both squares, the same relationship will exist between them for any other corresponding length. If a side of one square is twice the length of a side of the second square, the diagonal will also be twice as long. The ratio of the perimeters of the two squares is the same as the ratio of the sides. Therefore, the columns are equal. (C) is correct.

Step 4 Recap: QC Techniques

The Important Tips From This Step

➤ Memorize what the QC answer choices stand for. Know them cold by test day.

➤ Never mark choice (E) on a QC.

➤ Never pick choice (D) if both columns in a QC contain only numbers (no variables).

➤ If you can demonstrate two *different* relationships between the columns, choose choice (D).

➤ Use Kaplan's Top Four QC Strategies.

1. Make the terms in both columns similar.

2. Do the same thing to both columns.

3. Plug in two different sets of numbers, and compare columns for each.

4. Avoid traps. Don't assume that all variables are positive numbers, or that numbers that *look* alike, *are* alike.

✔ At-a-Glance

Below are the topics covered in today's lesson. Check each topic as you complete it. If you have time later, come back to any topics you've skipped or not understood entirely.

STEP 5 — BASIC VERBAL STRATEGIES

❏ How SAT Verbal Is Set Up
❏ How to Approach SAT Verbal
❏ Tapping Your Verbal Skills
❏ Decoding Strange Words on Test Day

STEP 6 — ANALOGY TECHNIQUES

❏ Building Bridges
❏ Kaplan's 3-Step Method
❏ Nine Classic Bridges

STEP 7 — CALCULATOR TECHNIQUES

❏ Should I Bring a Calculator?
❏ What Kind of Calculator Should I Bring?
❏ When Should I Use a Calculator?
❏ When Shouldn't I Use a Calculator?
❏ Two Common Calculator Mistakes

Step 5: Basic Verbal Strategies

SAT VERBAL ISN'T THE SUM OF ALL KNOWLEDGE ABOUT LANGUAGE

Linguists spend their entire lives studying the intricacies of language. But you don't have a lifetime to prepare for SAT Verbal. You have a week. Well, don't sweat it. There's a world of things about language that the test makers do *not* care about. The SAT, for instance, doesn't test spelling or grammar. It doesn't test your knowledge of English literature or literary terms. It will never ask you to interpret a poem. No, SAT Verbal covers a fairly predictable, fairly limited body of skills and knowledge: vocabulary, verbal reasoning, and reading skills. *You can boost your score with just the material presented here.*

❑ HOW SAT VERBAL IS SET UP

There are three scored Verbal sections on the SAT. The breakdown of the questions goes like this:

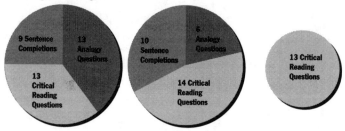

➤ one 30-minute section with 9 Sentence Completions, 13 Analogies, and 13 Critical Reading questions

➤ one 30-minute section with 10 Sentence Completions, 6 Analogies, and 14 Critical Reading questions

➤ one 15-minute section with 13 Critical Reading questions

The Sentence Completions and Analogies are arranged in order of difficulty. The first few questions in a set are meant to be fairly straightforward and manageable. The middle few questions will be a little harder, and the last few are the most difficult. Keep this in mind as you work.

Critical Reading is not arranged by difficulty. Whenever you find yourself beginning to spend too much time on a question, you should skip it and return to it later.

———————— ❖ ————————

**Learn the verbal question types now so you don't
have to figure them out on test day.**

———————— ❖ ————————

❏ HOW TO APPROACH SAT VERBAL

To do well on SAT Verbal, you need to be systematic in your approach to each question type and each of the three Verbal sections. Sentence Completions and Analogies are designed to be done relatively quickly. That means you can earn points fast, so you should do these first. Critical Reading takes a lot longer, so you can't just leave yourself five minutes to do a passage. *Remember, you earn just as many points for an easy question as you do for a hard one.*

❏ TAPPING YOUR SAT VERBAL SKILLS

Doing your best on SAT Verbal comes from knowing what to expect and knowing that you have the skills to handle it. You use words every day. You make your own ideas clear, and you understand and respond to those of others. In all of these cases — talking with friends or talking with teachers, reading a textbook or reading a billboard, listening to lyrics or listening to your SAT proctor's instructions — you take in limited information, process it through your own intellect and experience, and make sense of it. If you can learn to make the most of these skills, you can improve your Verbal score.

Here's how to apply those general points to the specifics of SAT Verbal:

VOCABULARY

You know how to read. You can explain the relationship between "kitten" and "cat" to a three-year-old. So what makes the Verbal section such a challenge? Vocabulary. You may have a solid understanding of a Critical Reading passage but then get thrown by one tough vocabulary word. You may know the relationship between the original pair of words in an Analogy, but have a tough time finding the answer because all the choices have words you've never seen before. You may know precisely what kind of word to fill in on a Sentence Completion, and then find that all the answer choices look like they're in a foreign language.

All three Verbal question types — Analogies, Sentence Completions, and Critical Reading — depend on your ability to work with unfamiliar words. You won't be asked to define words on the SAT. But you'll need to have a sense of their meaning in order to answer the questions.

There are two types of hard SAT words:
➤ unfamiliar words
➤ familiar words with unfamiliar meanings

Some words are hard because you haven't seen them before. The words "scintilla" or "circumlocution," for instance, are probably not part of your everyday vocabulary. But they might pop up on your SAT.

Easy words, like "recognize" or "appreciation," may also trip you up on test day because they have secondary meanings that you aren't used to. Analogies and Critical Reading in particular will throw you familiar words with unfamiliar meanings.

Those who prepare for the SAT months ahead of time study

word-roots and word lists to sharpen their vocabularies. But you can take a shortcut and get similar results. Here's how.

❏ DECODING STRANGE WORDS ON TEST DAY

Trying to learn every word that could possibly appear on the SAT is like trying to memorize the license-plate number of every car on the freeway. It's not much fun, it'll give you a headache, and you probably won't pull it off.

Even if you were to spend hours with flash cards, vocabulary tapes, and word lists, you'd be bound to face some mystery words on your SAT. No big deal. Just as you can use your basic multiplication skills to find the product of even the largest numbers, you can use what you know about words to focus on likely meanings of tough vocabulary words.

GO WITH YOUR HUNCHES
When you look at an unfamiliar word, your first reaction may be to say, "Don't know it. Gotta skip it." *Not so fast.* Vocabulary knowledge on the SAT is not an all-or-nothing proposition.

➤ Some words you know so well you can rattle off a dictionary definition of them.

➤ Some words you sort of know. You understand them when you see them in context, but don't feel confident using them yourself.

➤ Some words are vaguely familiar. You know you've heard them somewhere before.

1. Try to Recall Where You've Heard the Word Before
If you can recall a phrase in which the word appears, that may be enough to eliminate some answer choices, or even to zero in on the right answer.

Between the two villages was a deep——————through which passage was difficult and hazardous.

(A) precipice

(B) beachhead

(C) quagmire

(D) market

(E) prairie

To answer this question, it helps to know the word "quagmire." You may remember "quagmire" from news reports referring to "a foreign policy quagmire" or "a quagmire of financial indebtedness." If you can remember how "quagmire" was used, you'll have a rough idea of what it means, and you'll see it fits.

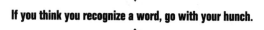

If you think you recognize a word, go with your hunch.

You may also be reminded of the word "mire," as in "We got mired in the small details and never got to the larger issue." Sounds something like "stuck," right? You don't need an exact definition. A quagmire is a situation that's difficult to get out of, so (C) is correct. (Literally, a quagmire is a soft, spongy, easy-to-get-stuck-in land.)

Use common word associations and phrases to unlock difficult words.

2. Decide if the Word Has a Positive or Negative "Charge"

Simply knowing that you're dealing with a positive or negative word can earn you points on the SAT.

Look at the word "cantankerous." Say it to yourself. Can you guess whether it's positive or negative? Often words that sound harsh have a negative meaning while smooth-sounding words tend to have positive meanings. If "cantankerous" sounded negative to you, you were right. It means "disagreeable" or "difficult to deal with."

You can also use prefixes and roots to help determine a word's charge. "Mal-," "de-," "dis-," "un-," "in-," "im-," "a-," and "mis-" often indicate a negative, while "pro-," "ben-," and "magn-" are often positives.

Not all SAT words sound positive or negative; some sound neutral. But if you can define the charge, you can probably eliminate some answer choices on that basis alone.

❖

Trust your sense of an unfamiliar word's "charge."

❖

He seemed at first to be honest and loyal, but before long it was necessary to——— him for his ——— behavior.

(A) admonish..steadfast

(B) extol..conniving

(C) reprimand..scrupulous

(D) exalt..insidious

(E) castigate..perfidious

You don't need an exact definition of the words that go in the blanks. The word "but" tells you all you need to know — that the words for both blanks have to be negative (to contrast with the positive words "honest" and "loyal"). So you scan the answer choices for a choice that contains two clearly negative words. (E) is right. "Castigate" means "punish or scold harshly," and "perfidious" means "disloyal" or "treacherous."

3. Use Your Foreign-Language Skills

Many of the roots you'll encounter in SAT words come from Latin. Spanish, French, and Italian also come from Latin, and have retained much of it in their modern forms. English is also a cousin to German and Greek. So if you don't recognize a word, you should try to remember if you know a similar word in another language.

Look at the word "carnal." Unfamiliar? What about "carne," as in "chili con carne"? "Carn" means "meat" or "flesh," which leads you straight to the meaning of "carnal": "pertaining to the flesh." You could decode carnivorous, meat-eating, in the same way.

Look for word elements you know from foreign languages.

---

4. When All Else Fails...

Eliminate choices that are clearly wrong and make an educated guess from the remaining choices.

➤ A wrong answer won't hurt you much.

➤ A right answer will help you a lot.

**Some choices on verbal questions will just sound wrong.
If you can eliminate at least one wrong-sounding choice, you
improve your chances of a correct guess.**

Step 5 Recap: Basic Verbal Strategies

The Important Tips From This Step

➤ Learn the verbal question types now so you don't have to figure them out on test day.

➤ If you think you recognize a word, go with your hunch.

➤ Use common word associations and phrases to unlock difficult words.

➤ Trust your sense of an unfamiliar word's "charge."

➤ Look for word elements you know from foreign languages.

➤ Some choices on verbal questions will just sound wrong. If you can eliminate at least one wrong-sounding choice, you improve your chances of a correct guess.

Step 6: Analogy Techniques

ANALOGIES ARE NOT A DISEASE

Analogies may seem frightening at first because they don't look like anything you've ever done before. But once you get familiar with the format, you'll find there's a simple method for mastering this question type. In fact, short-term prepping often gains you more points on Analogies than on any other Verbal question type. You can even learn to get the Analogy right when you don't know what all the words mean.

STATISTIC: The 19 Analogies count for about one-fourth of your verbal score.

❏ The Format

There are 19 Analogies on the SAT, and they are among the quickest 19 questions on the test. You'll probably see one set of 13 and one set of six. Each 30-minute Verbal section contains a set of Analogies. The directions will read something like those on the next page:

Choose the lettered pair of words that is related in the same way as the pair in capital letters.

EXAMPLE

FLAKE:SNOW::
(A) storm:hail
(B) drop:rain
(C) field:wheat
(D) stack:hay
(E) cloud:fog

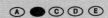

The key to the instructions is the word "related." Your job is to figure out which pair of words among your choices has the same relationship as the pair of stem words (the words in capital letters). In this example, the answer above is (B). A FLAKE is a small unit of SNOW, just as a drop is a small unit of rain.

❏ BUILD BRIDGES

In every Analogy question, there is a strong, definite connection between the two stem words. Your task is to identify this relationship and then look for a similar relationship among the answer pairs.

What makes a strong, definite relationship?

➤ The words "library" and "book" have a strong, definite connection. A library is defined as a place where books are kept. LIBRARY:BOOK could be a question stem.

➤ The words "library" and "child" do not have a strong, definite connection. A child may or may not have anything to do with a library. LIBRARY:CHILD would probably not be a question stem.

The best way to pinpoint the relationship between the stem words is to "build a bridge." A bridge is a short sentence that relates the two words. Often, a bridge reads like a definition of one of the two words. For instance: "A LIBRARY is a place where BOOKS are kept."

The ability to make up such sentences — to build bridges — is fundamental to Analogy success. Your bridge needs to capture the strong, definite connection between the words.

❖

Always build a bridge between Analogy stem words.

❖

❑ KAPLAN'S 3-STEP METHOD FOR ANALOGIES

1. Build a bridge between the stem words.
2. Plug in the answer choices.
3. Adjust your bridge, if you need to.

Here's an Analogy stem. We've left out the answer choices because you need to focus first on the stem.

LILY:FLOWER::

1. Build a Bridge.
The best bridge here is "A LILY is a type of FLOWER."

2. Plug in the Answer Choices.
Here is the complete question:

LILY:FLOWER::

- (A) rose:thorn
- (B) cocoon:butterfly
- (C) brick:building
- (D) maple:tree
- (E) sky:airplane

Take your bridge and plug in answer choices (A) through (E). If only one pair fits, it's the answer.

> HINT: Be sure to try all five choices. And don't be distracted
> by choices whose subject resembles that of the stem words.
> Unless the pair in the choice has the same relationship as the
> stem pair, it's wrong.

Here's how plugging in the answer choices works:
(A) A rose is a type of thorn? No.
(B) A cocoon is a type of butterfly? No.
(C) A brick is a type of building? No.
(D) A maple is a type of tree? Yes.
(E) A sky is a type of airplane? No.

Since only one choice fits our bridge, the answer is clearly (D).

3. Adjust Your Bridge If You Need To
If no answer choice seems to fit, your bridge is too specific, and you
should go back and adjust it. If more than one answer choice fits, your
bridge is not specific enough. Look at this example.

SNAKE:SLITHER::
(A) egg:hatch
(B) wolf:howl
(C) rabbit:hop
(D) turtle:snap
(E) tarantula:bite

With a simple bridge, such as "A SNAKE SLITHERs," you'd
have a hard time finding the answer. All the answer choices make
sense: An egg hatches; a wolf howls; a rabbit hops; a turtle snaps; a
tarantula bites. Don't worry. Go back to step one and build another
bridge, this time making it more specific. Think about what SLITHER

means.

New bridge: A SNAKE SLITHERs to get around.

(A) An egg hatches to get around? No.

(B) A wolf howls to get around? No.

(C) A rabbit hops to get around? Yes.

(D) A turtle snaps to get around? No.

(E) A tarantula bites to get around? No.

Four noes and one yes: The answer is (C).

> HINT: *If no answer fits, build a broader bridge; if too many fit, build a narrower bridge. Remember, only one answer choice should be able to "go across" the bridge.*

WHAT PART OF SPEECH IS A STEM WORD?

Occasionally, you might have to take a quick peek at the answer choices before you can build a bridge for the stem. The part of speech of a stem word may be ambiguous. When you're not sure whether a stem word is a noun, a verb, an adjective, or an adverb, look at the words directly beneath that stem word.

> HINT: *The words in a vertical row are all the same part of speech.*

For example, you might see this:

VERB:NOUN::
(A) verb:noun
(B) verb:noun
(C) verb:noun
(D) verb:noun
(E) verb:noun

but on an SAT Analogy you'll never see this:

NOUN:NOUN::
(A) verb:noun
(B) noun:noun
(C) verb:verb
(D) verb:noun
(E) verb:noun

To establish a stem word's part of speech, you don't usually have to look at more than one or two choices.

———————— ❖ ————————

Look at the choices if you don't know the part of speech of an ambiguous stem word.

———————— ❖ ————————

How would you think through the following example?

PINE:DESIRE::
(A) laugh:sorrow
(B) drink:thirst
(C) watch:interest
(D) listen:awe
(E) starve:hunger

The first thing you think of when you read PINE is the tree. But you can't build a bridge between a tree with needlelike leaves and DESIRE. So PINE has to be another part of speech. A glance at the answer choices below PINE ("laugh," "drink," "watch," "listen," and "starve") tells you that PINE is being used as a verb (since "listen" and "starve" can only be verbs).

What about DESIRE? It could be a noun or a verb, but the answer choices beneath it ("sorrow," "thirst," "interest," "awe," and "hunger") tell you it's used as a noun.

You've probably heard of someone pining away from unrequited love. As a verb, PINE means "to yearn or suffer from longing." A good bridge would be "to PINE is to suffer from extreme DESIRE." Plugging in the answer choices, you get:

(A) To laugh is to suffer from extreme sorrow? No.
(B) To drink is to suffer from extreme thirst? No.
(C) To watch is to suffer from extreme interest? No.
(D) To listen is to suffer from extreme awe? No.
(E) To starve is to suffer from extreme hunger? Yes.

Once again, four noes and one yes; the answer is (E).

------------------ ❖ ------------------

Use the Kaplan 3-Step Method for Analogies:
1. Build a bridge.
2. Plug in the answer choices.
3. Adjust your bridge if you need to.

------------------ ❖ ------------------

❑ NINE CLASSIC BRIDGES

It's easier to build bridges when you know the types of bridges that have appeared on the SAT in the past. While no one can give you a list of the words that will appear on SAT Analogies, you can learn what types of relationships to expect. The classic bridges below appear repeatedly on the SAT.

> HINT: *Learn to recognize common types of bridges that connect stem words on the SAT. They can speed you to the right answer.*

Classic bridges may take different forms, depending on what parts of speech are used. But the underlying concepts are what matter. Here are examples of nine classic types. Try to know these, or at least learn to recognize them, by test day.

Bridge Type #1: DESCRIPTION

In many Analogies, one stem word is a person, place, or thing, and the other word is a characteristic of that person, place, or thing. Look at these examples:

PAUPER:POOR — A PAUPER is always POOR.

GENIUS:INTELLIGENT — A GENIUS is always INTELLI-GENT.

This classic bridge can also describe a person, place, or thing by what it is *not*.

PAUPER:WEALTHY — A PAUPER is never WEALTHY.

GENIUS:STUPID — A GENIUS is never STUPID.

TRY IT YOURSELF

Here are more classic bridges. Fill in each blank with a stem word that will complete the bridge. There is more than one way to fill in each blank. The important thing is to get the right idea.

Bridge Type #2: CHARACTERISTIC ACTIONS

An INSOMNIAC can't ———.

A GLUTTON likes to ———.

Bridge Type #3: LACK

Something MURKY lacks ———.

A PESSIMIST lacks ———.

Bridge Type #4: CATEGORIES

MEASLES is a type of ———.

A BARRACUDA is a type of ———.

Bridge Type #5: SIZE/DEGREE
To SPEAK very quietly is to ———.
To LIKE strongly is to ———.

Bridge Type #6: CAUSING/STOPPING
A REMEDY stops or cures an ———.
An OBSTACLE prevents ———.

Bridge Type #7: PLACES
A JUDGE works in a ———.
A PLAY is performed on a ———.

Bridge Type #8: FUNCTION
GILLS are used for ———.
A PAINTBRUSH is used to ———.

Bridge Type #9: PART/WHOLE
An ARMY is made up of ———.
A CROWD is made up of many ———.

SUGGESTED ANSWERS TO BRIDGE TYPES

Your answers may vary from our suggested answers. As long as you recognized the relationship, that's okay.

CHARACTERISTIC ACTIONS
An INSOMNIAC can't SLEEP.
A GLUTTON likes to EAT.

LACK

Something MURKY lacks CLARITY.

A PESSIMIST lacks HOPE.

CATEGORIES

MEASLES is a type of ILLNESS.

A BARRACUDA is a type of FISH.

SIZE/DEGREE

To SPEAK very quietly is to WHISPER.

To LIKE strongly is to LOVE (or ADORE).

CAUSING/STOPPING

A REMEDY stops or cures an ILLNESS.

An OBSTACLE prevents PROGRESS (or PASSAGE).

PLACES

A JUDGE works in a COURTROOM.

A PLAY is performed on a STAGE (or in a THEATER).

FUNCTION

GILLS are used for BREATHING.

A PAINTBRUSH is used to PAINT.

PART/WHOLE

An ARMY is made up of SOLDIERS.

A CROWD is made up of many PEOPLE.

---❖---

**Learn to recognize the classic types of bridges
used in Analogy questions.**

---❖---

Now that you've got a handle on Analogies, try the pop quiz on the next page.

10 questions
5 minutes

1. COPPER:METAL::
   - (A) grain:sand
   - (B) helium:gas
   - (C) stem:flower
   - (D) tree:trunk
   - (E) stone:clay

2. BROOM:DIRT::
   - (A) brush:bristles
   - (B) fork:plate
   - (C) rake:leaves
   - (D) mirror:face
   - (E) scissors:blades

3. COWARD:BRAVERY::
   - (A) eccentric:conformity
   - (B) hero:fortitude
   - (C) prophet:vision
   - (D) sage:wisdom
   - (E) comedian:humor

4. REVERE:ADMIRE::
   - (A) cherish:conceive
   - (B) release:reject
   - (C) guess:solve
   - (D) propose:change
   - (E) despise:disdain

5. PERPLEXING:CONFUSION::
   (A) appalling:dismay
   (B) static:change
   (C) unpleasant:chaos
   (D) dignified:pride
   (E) grave:regret

6. AMUSING:MIRTH::
   (A) ailing:health
   (B) painful:sympathy
   (C) optimistic:objectivity
   (D) protective:insecurity
   (E) terrifying:fear

7. FOOD:MENU::
   (A) accounting:inventory
   (B) index:foreword
   (C) silverware:spoon
   (D) merchandise:catalogue
   (E) films:credits

8. IMPERCEPTIBLE:DETECT::
   (A) fundamental:begin
   (B) inconceivable:imagine
   (C) rugged:seize
   (D) costly:overcharge
   (E) immense:notice

9. PERSEVERE:DOGGED::
   (A) comply:obedient
   (B) inspire:pompous
   (C) hesitate:reckless
   (D) speak:laconic
   (E) retard:expeditious

10. ENTHRALLING:TEDIUM::
   (A) witty:frivolity
   (B) insipid:appetite
   (C) glaring:illumination
   (D) wearisome:redundancy
   (E) trite:originality

Explanations

1. (B) – Copper is a kind of metal.
2. (C) – A broom is used to clear away dirt.
3. (A) – A coward does not display bravery.
4. (E) – To revere is to admire very much.
5. (A) – Something that is perplexing causes confusion.
6. (E) – Something that is amusing causes mirth.
7. (D) – A menu is a list of available food.
8. (B) – If something is imperceptible, you cannot detect it.
9. (A) – A dogged person is one who perseveres.
10. (E) – Something that is enthralling lacks tedium.

Step 6 Recap: Analogy Techniques

The Important Tips From This Step

➤ Always build a bridge between Analogy stem words.

➤ Look at the choices if you don't know the part of speech of an ambiguous stem word.

➤ Use the Kaplan 3-Step Method for Analogies:

1. Build a bridge.

2. Plug in the answer choices.

3. Adjust your bridge, if you need to.

➤ Learn to recognize the classic types of bridges used in Analogy questions.

Step 7: Calculator Techniques

YOUR CALCULATOR IS NOT ALWAYS YOUR FRIEND

You are allowed to use a calculator on the SAT. That's a mixed blessing. The good news is that you can do computation faster. The bad news is that you may be tempted to waste time using a calculator on questions that shouldn't involve lengthy computation.

Remember, you never *need* a calculator to solve an SAT problem. If you ever find yourself doing extensive calculation — elaborate division or long drawn-out multiplication — stop and look again, because you probably missed a shortcut.

❏ SHOULD I BRING A CALCULATOR?

You definitely want to bring your calculator on test day. By zeroing in on the parts of problems that need calculation, you can increase your score and save yourself time on the SAT by using your calculator.

---------- ❖ ----------

Yes, bring a calculator, but don't overuse it.

---------- ❖ ----------

❏ WHAT KIND OF CALCULATOR SHOULD I BRING?

The best calculator to bring is one you're comfortable with. The most important thing is not how fancy your calculator is, but how good you are at using it. *If you don't have a calculator now, buy one right away, and practice using it between now and test day.* Remember that you won't be doing logs, trig functions, or preprogrammed formulas on the SAT.

You can use just about any small calculator except

➤ a calculator that prints out your calculations
➤ a hand-held minicomputer or a laptop computer

➤ any calculator with a typewriter keypad
➤ a calculator with an angled readout screen

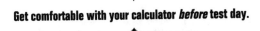

Get comfortable with your calculator *before* test day.

❏ WHEN SHOULD I USE A CALCULATOR?

Calculators help the most on Grid-ins and the least on QCs.

The reason for this is that QCs are designed to be done very quickly, and never involve much computation; if you think you need a calculator on them, you're missing something. Both Grid-ins and Regular Math will sometimes involve computation — never as the most important part of the question, but often as a final step.

Since Grid-ins, as we'll see, don't give you answer choices to choose from, it's especially important to be sure of your work. Calculators can help you check your work and avoid careless errors.

Remember, a calculator can be useful when used selectively and strategically. Not all parts of a problem will necessarily be easier with a calculator. Consider this problem:

> If four grams of cadmium yellow pigment can make 3 kilograms of cadmium yellow oil paint, how many kilograms of paint could be produced from 86 grams of pigment?

This word problem has two steps. Step one is to set up the following proportion:

$$\frac{4\,\text{gm}}{3\,\text{kg}} = \frac{86\,\text{gm}}{x\,\text{kg}}$$

A little algebraic engineering tells you that:

$$x\,\text{kg} = \frac{3\,\text{kg} \times 86\,\text{gm}}{4\,\text{gm}}$$

Third Day / Step 7: Calculator Techniques

Here's where you whip out that calculator. This problem has now been reduced down to pure calculation: $(3 \times 86) \div 4 = 64.5$.

❑ WHEN SHOULDN'T I USE A CALCULATOR?

Don't be fooled. On most SAT problems you may be tempted to use your calculator, but many questions will be easier without it. That's particularly true of QCs.

Consider this problem:

Column A	Column B
$\frac{5}{8} + \frac{8}{15}$	$\frac{4}{9} + \frac{10}{21}$

Sure, you could grab your calculator and divide out those fractions. You could then calculate the new values and compare the columns. But why bother?

If you just compare these terms to $\frac{1}{2}$ you'll be out of this problem much faster. After all, $\frac{5}{8}$ and $\frac{8}{15}$ from column A are both greater than $\frac{1}{2}$, and $\frac{4}{9}$ and $\frac{10}{21}$ (from column B) are both less than $\frac{1}{2}$. Quantity A must be greater.

Using your calculator would have slowed you down.

Be careful on non-QC questions, too. Consider this:

If $x^2 \times 8^2 = 49 \times 64 \times 81$, $x^2 =$
(A) 49^2
(B) 56^2
(C) 63^2
(D) 72^2
(E) 81^2

Now if you punch in $49 \times 64 \times 81$ you'll get 254,016. But that won't be too helpful. Look at the answer choices! Instead, realize that:

$$(x^2) \times 8^2 = (49 \times 81) \times 64.$$

8^2 is the same thing as 64, so get rid of the 64's on both sides. You get:

$$x^2 = 49 \times 81.$$

So that's $x^2 = 7^2 \times 9^2$

or $x^2 = 7 \times 7 \times 9 \times 9$

which is 63×63 or 63^2.

No calculator required.

———————— ❖ ————————

Don't let your calculator blind you to the fast solution to a question.

———————— ❖ ————————

❏ TWO COMMON CALCULATOR MISTAKES

CALCULATOR MISTAKE #1: CALCULATING BEFORE YOU THINK

On the Grid-in problem below, how should (and shouldn't) you use your calculator?

> The sum of all the integers from 1 to 44, inclusive, is subtracted from the sum of all the integers from 7 to 50, inclusive. What is the result?

The Wrong Approach:

➤ Grab calculator.

➤ Punch in all the numbers.

➤ Put down answer and hope you didn't hit any wrong buttons.

Faced with this problem, you might be tempted to punch in all the numbers from 1 to 44, find their sum, then do the same for numbers 7 through 50, and subtract the first sum from the second. But doing that means punching 252 keys. The odds are you'll slip up somewhere, hit the wrong key, and get the wrong answer. Even if you don't, punching in all those numbers takes too much time.

The Kaplan Approach:

➤ Think first.

➤ Decide on the best way to solve the problem.

➤ Only then, use your calculator.

The right approach is to think first. The amount of computation involved in directly solving this tells you that there must be an easier way. You'll see this if you realize that both sums are of the same number of consecutive integers. Each integer in the first sum has a corresponding integer 6 greater than it in the second sum:

1	7
+2	+8
+3	+9
.	.
.	.
.	.
+42	+48
+43	+49
+44	+50
=	=

How many pairs of integers are there? As we'll see in the Math

Traps step, the way to find the number of integers in a consecutive series is to subtract the smallest from the largest and add 1 (44 − 1 = 43; 43 + 1 = 44 OR 50 − 7 = 43; 43 + 1 = 44) So there are 44 pairs of integers that are 6 apart.

Therefore, the total difference between the two sums will be the difference between each pair of integers times the number of pairs.

———————— ❖ ————————

Think before you punch buttons.

———————— ❖ ————————

Now take out your calculator, punch "6 × 44 =," and get the correct answer of 264, with little or no time wasted.

> WARNING: *If you're punching buttons for long stretches at a time, you're approaching the problem the wrong way.*

CALCULATOR MISTAKE #2: FORGETTING THE ORDER OF OPERATIONS

Watch out. Even when you use your calculator, you can't just enter numbers in the order they appear on the page — you've got to follow the order of operations. This is a very simple error, but it can cost you lots of points. The order of operations is "PEMDAS," which stands for:

Parentheses
Exponents
Multiplication
Division
Addition
Subtraction

That means you do whatever is in parentheses first, then deal with exponents, then multiplication and division, and finally addition and subtraction.

For example, say you want to find the value of the expression

$$\frac{x^2 + 1}{x + 3} \quad \text{when } x = 7$$

If you just punched in "7 × 7 + 1 ÷ 7 + 3 =" you would get the wrong answer.

The correct way to work it out is

$(7^2 + 1) \div (7 + 3) = (7 \times 7 + 1) \div (7 + 3) = (49 + 1) \div 10$
$= 50 \div 10 = 5$

———————— ❖ ————————

**Remember PEMDAS (the order of operations)
when making calculations. And make sure you know
how your calculator handles multi-step calculations.**

———————— ❖ ————————

Combining a calculator with an understanding of when and how to use it can help you boost your score.

Step 7 Recap: Calculator Techniques

The Important Tips From This Step:

➤ Yes, bring a calculator, but don't overuse it.

➤ Get comfortable with your calculator *before* test day.

➤ Don't let your calculator blind you to the fast solution to a question.

➤ Think before you punch buttons.

➤ Remember PEMDAS (the order of operations) when making calculations. And make sure you know how your calculator handles multi-step calculations.

✔ At-a-Glance

Below are the topics covered in today's lesson. Check each topic as you complete it. If you have time later, come back to any topics you've skipped or not understood entirely.

STEP 8 — CLASSIC MATH TECHNIQUES

- ☐ Remainders
- ☐ Averages
- ☐ Ratios
- ☐ Rates
- ☐ Percents
- ☐ Simultaneous Equations
- ☐ Symbolism
- ☐ Special Triangles

(Time: 60 minutes)

STEP 9 — SENTENCE COMPLETION TECHNIQUES

- ☐ The Format
- ☐ Kaplan's 4-Step Method
- ☐ Picking Up on Clues

(Time: 60 minutes)

Step 8: Classic Math Techniques

THE MATH YOU KNEW BUT PROBABLY FORGOT

There are certain types of math skills that are tested again and again on the SAT. You almost certainly learned these skills in your math classes over the years, but are they still as sharp as they should be?

What you don't want to do is spend valuable time on test day dredging your memory for techniques you were taught years ago. Now is the time to sharpen up those rusty skills. In this step, we'll give you a quick brush-up on some of the SAT-makers' favorite Math question types, along with Kaplan's classic pointers for solving them. These are by no means exhaustive discussions, but they should be enough to clear away a few mental cobwebs.

> STATISTIC: *The 35 Regular Math questions count for just over one-half of your Math score.*

The following techniques work for all SAT Math questions, whether Regular Math, QC, or Grid-in.

☐ CLASSIC MATH TECHNIQUE #1: REMAINDERS

Remainder questions can be easier than they look. You might think you have to solve for a certain value, but often you don't.

> **EXAMPLE**
>
> When n is divided by 7, the remainder is 4. What is the remainder when $2n$ is divided by 7?
>
> (A) 0
>
> (B) 1
>
> (C) 2
>
> (D) 3
>
> (E) 4

The question above doesn't depend on knowing the value of n. In fact, n has an infinite number of possible values.

> HINT: *The easy way to solve this kind of problem is to pick a number for* n.

Which number should you pick? Since the remainder when n is divided by 7 is 4, pick any multiple of 7 and add 4. The easiest multiple to work with is 7. So, $7 + 4 = 11$. Use 11 for n.

Plug 11 into the question and see what happens:

➤ What is the remainder when $2n$ is divided by 7?

-the remainder when $2(11)$ is divided by 7?

-the remainder when 22 is divided by 7?

$\frac{22}{7} = 3$ remainder 1

The remainder is 1 when $n = 11$. So the answer is (B). The remainder will also be 1 when $n = 18$, 25, or 46.

Plug in numbers when solving remainder questions.

❖

❑ CLASSIC MATH TECHNIQUE #2: AVERAGES

EXAMPLE

The average weight of 5 dogs in a certain kennel is 32 pounds. If 4 of the dogs weigh 25, 27, 19, and 35 pounds, what is the weight of the fifth dog?

(A) 28

(B) 32

(C) 49

(D) 54

(E) 69

Instead of giving you a list of values to plug into the average formula, SAT average questions often put a slight spin on the problem. They tell you the average of a group of terms and ask you to find the value of a missing term.

HINT: *Work with the sum.*

Let x = the weight of the fifth dog. Plug this into the average formula which is:

$$\text{Average} = \frac{\text{Sum of Terms}}{\text{Number of Terms}}$$

$$32 = \frac{25 + 27 + 19 + 35 + x}{5}$$

$$32 \times 5 = 25 + 27 + 19 + 35 + x$$

So the average weight of the dogs, times the number of dogs, equals the total weight of the dogs. The new formula is: Average × Number of Terms=Sum of Terms.

Remember this manipulation of the average formula so that, whenever you know the average of a group of terms and the number of terms, you can find the total sum.

Now you can solve for the weight of the fifth dog:

$$32 \times 5 = 25 + 27 + 19 + 35 + x$$
$$160 = 106 + x$$
$$54 = x$$

So the weight of the fifth dog is 54 pounds, choice (D).

———— ❖ ————

Remember that Average × Number of Terms = Sum of Terms.

———— ❖ ————

❏ CLASSIC MATH TECHNIQUE #3: RATIOS

EXAMPLE

Out of every 50 chips produced in a certain factory, 20 are defective. What is the ratio of nondefective chips produced to defective chips produced?

(A) 2:5

(B) 3:5

(C) 2:3

(D) 3:2

(E) 5:2

The key here is that the test makers try to get you to set up the wrong ratio.

HINT: Identify the parts and the whole in the problem.

Find the parts and the whole in the problem. In this case the total number of chips is the whole, and the number of nondefective chips and the number of defective chips are the parts that make up this whole.

You're given a part-to-whole ratio (the ratio of defective chips to all chips) and asked to find a part-to-part ratio (the ratio of nondefective chips to defective chips).

If 20 chips out of every 50 are defective, the remaining 30 chips must be nondefective. So the part-to-part ratio of nondefective to defective chips is $\frac{30}{20}$, or $\frac{3}{2}$, which is equivalent to 3:2, answer choice (D).

If you hadn't identified the part and the whole first it would be easy to get confused and compare a part to the whole, like the ratios in answer choices (A), (B), and (E).

This approach also works for ratio questions where you need to find actual quantities. For example:

Out of every 5 chips produced in a certain factory, 2 are defective. If 2,200 chips were produced, how many were defective?

Here you need to find a quantity, the number of defective chips.

HINT: *If you're looking for the actual quantities in a ratio, set up and solve a proportion.*

You're given a part-to-whole ratio (the ratio of defective chips to all chips), and the total number of chips produced. You can find the answer by setting up and solving a proportion:

$$\frac{\text{Number of defective chips}}{\text{Total number of chips}} = \frac{2}{5} = \frac{x}{2,200}$$

x = number of defective chips
$5x = 4,400$ (by cross-multiplying $\frac{2}{5} = \frac{x}{2,200}$)
$x = 880$ (by dividing both sides by 5)

HINT: *Remember that ratios only compare relative size; they don't tell you the actual quantities involved.*

———————— ❖ ————————

Distinguish clearly between the parts and the whole in ratio problems.

———————— ❖ ————————

❏ CLASSIC MATH TECHNIQUE #4: RATES

EXAMPLE

If 8 oranges cost a dollars, b oranges would cost how many dollars?

(A) $8ab$

(B) $\frac{8a}{b}$

(C) $\frac{8}{ab}$

(D) $\frac{a}{8b}$

(E) $\frac{ab}{8}$

A rate is a ratio that compares quantities measured in different units. In the problem above, the units are dollars and oranges.

What makes this rate problem difficult is the presence of variables. It's hard to get a clear picture of the relationship between the units.

HINT: *Pick numbers for the variables to make the relationship between the units clearer.*

Pick numbers for a and b that are easy to work with in the problem.

Let $a = 16$. Then 8 oranges cost $16. So the cost per orange at this rate = $\frac{\$16}{8 \text{ oranges}}$ = $2 per orange.

Let $b = 5$. So the cost of 5 oranges at this rate is 5 oranges × 2 dollars per orange = $10.

Now plug in $a = 16$ and $b = 5$ into the answer choices to see which one gives you a value of 10.

Choice (A): $8 \times 16 \times 5 = 640$. Eliminate.

Choice (B): $\frac{8 \times 16}{5} = \frac{128}{5}$. Eliminate.

Choice (C): $\frac{8}{16 \times 5} = \frac{1}{10}$. Eliminate.

Choice (D): $\frac{16}{8 \times 5} = \frac{2}{5}$. Eliminate.

Choice (E): $\frac{16 \times 5}{8} = 10$.

Since (E) is the only one that gives the correct value, it is correct.

Make rates concrete by plugging in numbers for variables.

❑ CLASSIC MATH TECHNIQUE #5: PERCENTS

EXAMPLE

Last year Julie's annual salary was $20,000. This year's raise brings her to an annual salary of $25,000. If she gets a raise of the same percentage every year, what will her salary be next year?

(A) $27,500

(B) $30,000

(C) $31,250

(D) $32,500

(E) $35,000

In percent problems, you're usually given two pieces of information and asked to find the third. When you see a percent problem, remember:

➤ If you are solving for a percent:

$$\text{Percent} = \frac{\text{Part}}{\text{Whole}}$$

➤ If you need to solve for a part:

$$\text{Percent} \times \text{Whole} = \text{Part}$$

This problem asks for Julie's projected salary for next year — that is, her current salary plus her next raise.

You know last year's salary ($20,000) and you know this year's salary ($25,000), so you can find the difference between the two salaries:

$25,000 - $20,000 = $5,000 =$ her raise.

Now find the percent of her raise, by using the formula $\text{Percent} = \frac{\text{Part}}{\text{Whole}}$.

Since Julie's raise was calculated on last year's salary, divide by $20,000.

> HINT: *Be sure you know which whole to plug in. Here you're looking for a percentage of $20,000, not of $25,000.*

Percent raise = $\frac{\$5000}{\$20,000} = \frac{1}{4}$ = 25%.

You know she will get the same percent raise next year, so solve for the part. Use the formula Percent × Whole = Part.

Her raise next year will be 25% × $25,000 = $\frac{1}{4}$ × 25,000 = $6,250.

Add that sum to this year's salary and you have her projected salary:

$25,000 + $6,250 = $31,250, or answer choice (C).

Make sure you change the percent to either a fraction or a decimal before beginning calculations.

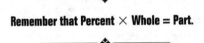

Remember that Percent × Whole = Part.

❑ CLASSIC MATH TECHNIQUE #6: SIMULTANEOUS EQUATIONS

EXAMPLE

If $p + 2q = 14$ and $3p + q = 12$, then $p =$

(Note: This is a Grid-in, so there are no choices.)

In order to get a numerical value for each variable, you need as many different equations as there are variables to solve for. So, if you have two variables, you need two independent equations.

You could tackle this problem by solving for one variable in terms of the other, and then plugging this expression into the other equation. But the simultaneous equations that appear on the SAT can usually be handled in an easier way.

HINT: *Combine the equations — by adding or subtracting them — to cancel out all but one of the variables.*

You can't eliminate p or q by adding or subtracting the equations in their present form.

But if you multiply the second equation by 2:
$2(3p + q) = 2(12)$
$6p + 2q = 24$

Now when you subtract the first equation from the second, the qs will cancel out so you can solve for p:

$$6p + 2q = 24$$
$$-[p + 2q = 14]$$
$$\overline{}$$
$$5p + 0 = 10$$

If $5p = 10$, $p = 2$. On the answer sheet, you would grid in the answer 2.

❖

Add and subtract simultaneous equations to cancel out variables.

❖

❑ CLASSIC MATH TECHNIQUE #7: SYMBOLISM

EXAMPLE

If $a \star b = \sqrt{a+b}$ for all non-negative numbers, what is the value of $10 \star 6$?

(A) 0

(B) 2

(C) 4

(D) 8

(E) 16

You should be quite familiar with the arithmetic symbols $+$, $-$, $\times$, and $\div$. Finding the value of $10 + 2$, $18 - 4$, 4×9, or $96 \div 16$ is easy.

However, on the SAT, you may come across bizarre symbols. You may even be asked to find the value of $10 \star 2$, $5 \circledast 7$, $10 \bullet 6$, or $65 \blacklozenge 2$.

The SAT-makers put strange symbols in questions to confuse or unnerve you. Don't let them. The question stem always tells you what the strange symbol means. Although this type of question may look difficult, it is really an exercise in plugging in.

To solve, just plug in 10 for a and 6 for b into the expression $\sqrt{a+b}$. That equals $\sqrt{10+6}$, or $\sqrt{16}$ or 4: choice (C).

Plug in numbers for symbolism questions.

❏ CLASSIC MATH TECHNIQUE #8: SPECIAL TRIANGLES

EXAMPLE

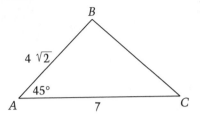

In the triangle above, what is the length of side *BC*?

(A) 4

(B) 5

(C) $4\sqrt{2}$

(D) 6

(E) $5\sqrt{2}$

HINT: Look for the special triangles in geometry problems.

Special triangles contain a lot of information. For instance, if you know the length of one side of a 30-60-90 triangle, you can easily work out the lengths of the others. Special triangles allow you to transfer one piece of information around the whole figure.

The following are the special triangles you should look for on the SAT. You don't have to memorize the ratios (they're listed in the instructions), but you should be familiar enough with them to recognize them when you see them.

Equilateral Triangles

All interior angles are 60° and all sides are of the same length.

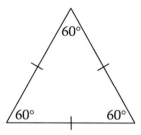

Isosceles Triangles

Two sides are of the same length, and the angles facing these sides are equal.

Right Triangles

These contain a 90° angle. The sides are related by the Pythagorean theorem: $a^2 + b^2 = c^2$ where a and b are the legs and c is the hypotenuse.

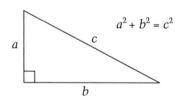

THE "SPECIAL" RIGHT TRIANGLES

Many triangle problems contain "special" right triangles, whose side lengths always come in predefined ratios. If you recognize them, you won't have to use the Pythagorean theorem to find the value of a missing side length.

The 3-4-5 Right Triangle

(Be on the lookout for multiples of 3-4-5 as well.)

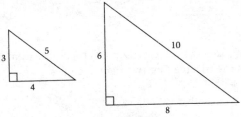

The Isosceles Right Triangle

(Note the side ratio: 1 to 1 to $\sqrt{2}$.)

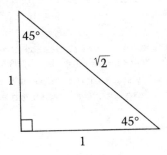

The 30-60-90 Right Triangle

(Note the side ratio: 1 to $\sqrt{3}$ to 2, and which side is opposite which angle.)

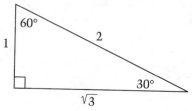

Getting back to our example, you can drop a vertical line from B to line AC. This divides the triangle into two right triangles.

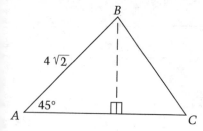

That means you know two of the angles in the triangle on the left: 90° and 45°. The third angle must also be 45°, so this is an isosceles right triangle, with sides in the ratio of 1 to 1 to $\sqrt{2}$. The hypotenuse here is $4\sqrt{2}$, so both legs have length 4. Filling this in, you have:

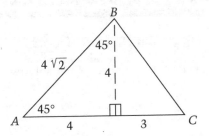

Now you can see that the legs of the smaller triangle on the right must be 4 and 3, making this a 3-4-5 right triangle, and the length of hypotenuse BC is 5. So choice (B) is correct.

———————❖———————

Learn how to use the properties of special types of triangles.

———————❖———————

Step 8 Recap: Classic Math Techniques

The Important Tips From This Step

➤ Plug in numbers when solving remainder questions.

➤ Remember that Average × Number of Terms = Sum of Terms

➤ Distinguish clearly between the parts and the whole in ratio problems.

➤ Make rates concrete by plugging in numbers for variables.

➤ Remember that Percent × Whole = Part.

➤ Add and subtract simultaneous equations to cancel out variables.

➤ Plug in numbers for symbolism questions.

➤ Learn how to use the properties of special types of triangles.

Step 9: Sentence Completion Techniques

FILLING IN THE BLANKS

Of all the Verbal question types, Sentence Completions are probably the most student-friendly. Unlike Analogies, they give you some context in which to think about vocabulary words, and unlike Critical Reading, they only require you to pay attention to a single sentence at a time.

> *STATISTIC: The 19 Sentence Completions count for about one-fourth of your verbal score.*

❏ THE FORMAT

There are 19 Sentence Completions in all on the SAT. You'll probably see one set of nine and one set of ten. They appear in both 30-minute Verbal sections. The instructions for Sentence Completions look something like those on the next page:

Select the lettered word or set of words that best completes the sentence.

EXAMPLE

Today's small, portable computers contrast markedly with the earliest electronic computers, which were ——————

(A) effective

(B) invented

(C) useful

(D) destructive

(E) enormous

 Ⓐ Ⓑ ⓒ Ⓓ ●

In the example, the new computers, which are small and portable, are *contrasted* with old computers. You can infer that the old computers must have been the opposite of small and portable, so (E), enormous, is right.

❏ KAPLAN'S 4-STEP METHOD FOR SENTENCE COMPLETIONS

Here's the basic method for Sentence Completions:

1. READ THE SENTENCE CAREFULLY

Think about the sentence before looking at the answer choices. Figure out what the sentence means, taking special note of clue words. A word like "but" tells you to expect a contrast coming up; a word like "moreover" tells you that what follows is a continuation of the same idea.

————————— ❖ —————————

Clue words like "and," "but," "such as," and "although" tell you how the parts of a sentence relate to each other.

————————— ❖ —————————

2. PREDICT THE ANSWER

Anticipate the words that go in the blanks. Do this before looking at the answer choices.

> *HINT: You don't have to make an exact prediction. A rough idea of the kind of word you need will do. It's often enough simply to predict whether the missing word is positive or negative.*

❖

Decide in advance what sort of word should fill the blank or blanks.

❖

3. SELECT THE BEST MATCH BY COMPARING YOUR PREDICTION WITH EACH ANSWER CHOICE

❖

Read every answer choice before deciding.

❖

4. READ THE SENTENCE WITH YOUR ANSWER CHOICE IN THE BLANK OR BLANKS

> *HINT: Only one choice will really make sense.*

If you've gone through the four steps and more than one choice seems possible, don't get stuck on the sentence. Eliminate whatever choices you can; guess; and move on. If a question really stumps you, circle it and come back when you're done with the section.

❖

Reread the sentence with your choice plugged in.

❖

Here's how the 4-Step Approach works on some examples.

EXAMPLE

Alligators, who bask in the sun for hours, appear to be ——— creatures, yet they are quite capable of sudden movement.

(A) active

(B) violent

(C) stern

(D) content

(E) sluggish

1. READ THE SENTENCE CAREFULLY, LOOKING FOR CLUE WORDS

"Yet" is a major clue. It tells you that the sentence switches direction midstream. The word in the blank must be something opposed to "sudden."

2. PREDICT THE WORD THAT GOES IN THE BLANK

You can guess that alligators seem like "lazy" or "idle" creatures.

3. COMPARE YOUR PREDICTION WITH EACH ANSWER CHOICE, AND PICK THE BEST MATCH

(A) "active" has nothing to do with being lazy or idle.

Neither does (B) "violent."

Neither does (C) "stern."

Neither does (D) "content."

But (E) "sluggish" means "inactive" or "slow-moving," so pick (E).

4. CHECK YOUR ANSWER BY PLUGGING IT INTO THE SENTENCE

Let's check: "Alligators, who bask in the sun for hours, appear to be sluggish creatures, yet they are quite capable of sudden movement."

Sounds good. None of the other choices works in the sentence, so (E)'s correct.

> HINT: Try to avoid reading the sentence five times, plugging in every answer choice. That method takes too much time and should only be used if you're stuck. Instead, think about the question before you look for the answer.

EXAMPLE

The king's ———— decisions as a diplomat and administrator led to his legendary reputation as a just and ———— ruler.

- (A) quick..capricious
- (B) equitable..wise
- (C) immoral..perceptive
- (D) generous..witty
- (E) clever..uneducated

---

1. READ THE SENTENCE CAREFULLY, LOOKING FOR CLUE WORDS

A big clue here is the phrase "led to." You know that the kind of decisions the king made gave him a reputation as a just and ———— ruler. So whatever goes in both blanks must be consistent with "just."

2. PREDICT THE WORD THAT GOES IN THE BLANK

Notice that both blanks must be similar in meaning. Because of his ———— decisions, the king is viewed as a just and ———— ruler. So if the king's decisions were good, he'd be remembered as a good ruler, and if his decisions were bad, he'd be remembered as a bad ruler. "Just," which means "fair," is a positive-sounding word; you can predict that both blanks will be similar in meaning, and that both will be positive words. Write a "+" in the blanks or over the columns of answer choices to remind you.

3. COMPARE YOUR PREDICTION WITH EACH ANSWER CHOICE, AND PICK THE BEST MATCH

One way to do this is to determine which answers are both positive and similar.

In (A), "quick" and "capricious" aren't both positive and similar. ("Capricious" means "erratic or fickle.")

In (B), "equitable" means "fair." "Equitable" and "wise" are similar, and they're both positive. When you plug them in, they make sense, so (B) looks right. But check out the others to be sure.

In (C), "immoral" and "perceptive" aren't similar at all. "Perceptive" is positive but "immoral" isn't.

In (D), "generous" and "witty" are both positive adjectives, but they aren't really similar and they don't make sense in the sentence. Generous decisions would not give one a reputation as a witty ruler.

In (E), "clever" and "uneducated" aren't similar. "Clever" is positive, but "uneducated" isn't.

4. CHECK YOUR ANSWER BY PLUGGING IT INTO THE SENTENCE

"The king's equitable decisions as a diplomat and administrator led to his legendary reputation as a just and wise ruler." (B) makes sense in the sentence. So (B)'s our answer.

❑ PICKING UP ON CLUES

To do well on Sentence Completions, you need to see how a sentence fits together. Clue words help you do that. The more clues you get, the clearer the sentence becomes, and the better you can predict what goes in the blanks.

What do we mean by clue words? Take a look at this example:

> Though some have derided it as ——, the search for extraterrestrial intelligence has actually become a respectable scientific endeavor.

Here, the word "though" is an important clue. "Though" contrasts the way some have derided, belittled, or ridiculed the search for extraterrestrial intelligence, with the fact that that search has become respectable. Another clue is "actually." "Actually" completes the contrast: *Though* some see the search one way, it has *actually* become respectable.

You know that whatever goes in the blank must complete the contrast implied by the word "though." So, to fill in the blank, you need a word that would be used to describe the opposite of "a respectable scientific endeavor." "Useless" or "trivial" would be a good prediction for the blank.

Try using clue words to predict the answers to the two questions below. First, look at the sentences without the answer choices and:

➤ Circle clue words.

➤ Think of a word or phrase that might go in each blank.

➤ Write your prediction below each sentence.

1. One striking aspect of Caribbean music is its —— of many African musical ——, such as call-and-response singing and polyrhythms.

   _____   _____

2. Although Cézanne was inspired by the Impressionists, he —— their emphasis on the effects of light and —— an independent approach to painting that emphasized form.

   _____   _____

Here are the same two questions with their answer choices (and with their clue words italicized). Now find the right answer to each question, referring to the predictions you just made.

1. One striking aspect of Caribbean music is its ———— of many
   African musical ————, *such as* call-and-response singing
   and polyrhythms.
   (A) recruitment..groups
   (B) proficiency..events
   (C) expectation..ideas
   (D) absorption..forms
   (E) condescension..priorities

2. *Although* Cézanne was inspired by the Impressionists,
   he ———— their emphasis on the effects of light and ————
   an independent approach to painting that emphasized
   form.
   (A) accepted..developed
   (B) rejected..evolved
   (C) encouraged..submerged
   (D dismissed..aborted
   (E) nurtured..founded

Circle clue words.

By the way, the answers to the two questions above are (D) and
(B). In question 1, "such as" tells you that the second blank must be
something (genres, practices, forms) of which call-and-response
singing and polyrhythms are examples. "Although" in question 2 tells
you that the first blank must contrast with Cezanne's being "inspired"
by the Impressionists.

Let's finish the day with a quiz to solidify what you've learned.

SENTENCE COMPLETIONS POP QUIZ

6 questions

4 minutes

1. In the years following World War II, almost all Canadian Inuits ——— their previously nomadic lifestyle; they now live in fixed settlements.

   (A) abandoned

   (B) continued

   (C) fashioned

   (D) preserved

   (E) rebuilt

2. A newborn infant's ——— skills are not fully ———, for it cannot discern images more than ten inches from its face.

   (A) perceptual..stimulated

   (B) visual..developed

   (C) descriptive..ripened

   (D) olfactory..shared

   (E) average..familiar

3. Some geysers erupt regularly, while others do so ———.

   (A) consistently

   (B) copiously

   (C) perennially

   (D) sporadically

   (E) violently

4. Because of the lead actor's ——— performance, the play received poor reviews from influential theater critics, and was canceled only one week after it opened.

   (A) erudite

   (B) corporeal

   (C) overwrought

   (D) fractious

   (E) resplendent

5. Sociologists have found that, paradoxically, many children of unorthodox, creative parents grow up to be rather tame ———.

   (A) idealists

   (B) conformists

   (C) individualists

   (D) alarmists

   (E) elitists

6. In Han mortuary art, the ——— and the ——— are combined; one tomb may contain eerie supernatural figures placed next to ordinary likenesses of government administrators at work.

   (A) fantastic..mundane

   (B) inventive..remorseful

   (C) illusory..derivative

   (D) enlightened..conservative

   (E) unique..historical

Explanations

1. (A)
The semicolon indicates that what follows — the statement that the Inuit now live in fixed settlements — is a continuation of the thought that came before. "Nomadic" means "wandering, transient," so, to be consistent, the first part of the sentence must say that the Inuit rejected, or abandoned, "their previously nomadic lifestyle."

2. (B)
"For" means "since" here, indicating that what follows is an explanation or clarification. What can be clarified by a statement that a newborn infant "cannot discern [perceive] images more than ten inches from its face"? The statement that the infant's ability to see things has not fully evolved. In other words, a newborn's visual skills are not fully developed. (In (D), olfactory means "relating to sense of smell.")

3. (D)
The clue words "while others" indicate contrast. If some geysers "erupt regularly," we can predict that these "others" do so irregularly. The best choice is (D): "sporadically" means "infrequently or irregularly."

4. (C)
The clue words "because of" signal an explanation. If the play "received poor reviews" and was canceled because of something about the lead actor's performance, that performance must have been quite bad. (C), overwrought — overdone, or excessively agitated — is one of two negative words in the answer choices, and the only one that could logically describe a performance ("fractious," choice (D), means "cranky" or "cantankerous").

5. (B)
"Paradoxically" (or, in other words, "contrary to what one would expect"), children of creative and unorthodox parents grow up to be

something other than creative and unorthodox. We need a word that contrasts with "creative and unorthodox" but goes along with "tame." (B) is the best choice: Conformists are people who follow established norms and customs without challenging anything or anyone.

6. (A)

Again, a semicolon indicates a continuation of the same thought. If the statement that "one tomb contains eerie supernatural figures" and "ordinary likenesses of government administrators" is supposed to continue the first part of the sentence, then it must be true that Han mortuary art combines the unearthly or bizarre with the ordinary or everyday. The best answer is (A): In Han art, the fantastic (eerie supernatural figures) and the mundane (administrators) are combined.

Step 9 Recap: Sentence Completion Techniques

The Important Tips From This Step:

➤ Use the Kaplan 4-Step Method for Sentence Completions:
1. Read the Sentence Carefully
2. Predict the Answer
3. Select the Best Match
4. Read the Sentence with your Answer Choice in the Blank or Blanks.

➤ Clue words like "and," "but," "such as," and "although" tell you how the parts of a sentence are related to each other.

➤ Decide in advance what sort of word should fill the blank or blanks.

➤ Read every answer choice before deciding.

➤ Reread the sentence with your choice plugged in.

➤ Circle clue words.

✔ At-a-Glance

Below are the topics covered in today's lesson. Check each topic as you complete it. If you have time later, come back to any topics you've skipped or not understood entirely.

STEP 10 — CRITICAL READING BASIC TECHNIQUES

❑ The Format
❑ How to Read a Passage
❑ Your Critical Reading Smarts
❑ The 5-Step Method
❑ Applying the 5-Step Method
(Time: 60 minutes)

STEP 11 — CRITICAL READING FOCUSED TECHNIQUES

❑ Big Picture Questions
❑ Little Picture Questions
❑ Vocabulary-in-Context Questions
❑ Paired Passages
❑ Special Timing Advice
(Time: 60 minutes)

Step 10: Critical Reading Basic Techniques

IF YOU CAN READ THIS MESSAGE, YOU CAN SUCCEED AT CRITICAL READING

Improving your Critical Reading score means building skills you have and applying them to the SAT. You don't need outside knowledge to answer the Critical Reading questions. And you don't need an amazing vocabulary, since unfamiliar terms will be defined for you. In fact, defining words from context is one of the things the SAT asks you to do — in Vocabulary-in-Context questions, which we'll cover in Step 11.

Critical Reading passages and questions are very predictable. You'll be given four reading passages, of 400 to 850 words each, drawn from the arts, humanities, social sciences, sciences, and fiction. One of these is a "paired passage" consisting of two related passages.

Most questions will ask about the overall tone and content of a passage, its details, and what it suggests. For paired passages, you'll also be asked to compare and contrast the related passages.

> *STATISTIC: The 40 Critical Reading questions count for over half of your verbal score.*

40 Critical Reading Questions

Critical Reading instructions are simple: "Answer questions based on what is stated or implied in the accompanying passage or passages." That's all the guidance the test makers give you. We'll give you more.

Each reading passage, first of all, begins with a brief introduction. Don't even think of skipping it.

---❖---

**Don't skip the brief introductions.
They'll help you focus your reading.**

---❖---

After the passage come the questions. Critical Reading questions have a specific order: The first few questions ask about the beginning of the passage, the last few about the end.

Questions following "paired passages" are also ordered: The first few questions ask about the first passage, the next few about the second passage, and the final ones about the passages as a pair.

Unlike all other kinds of questions on the SAT, Critical Reading questions are not ordered by difficulty. On Critical Reading, the location of a question tells you nothing about its potential difficulty. So don't get bogged down on a hard Critical Reading question. The next one might be a lot easier.

As we'll see, certain kinds of Critical Reading questions — Vocabulary-in-Context questions, for instance — can often be done easily and quickly, even if you haven't read the passage. These are the questions to seek out if you're running out of time.

HINT: *Critical Reading questions are* not *ordered by difficulty.*

❑ HOW TO READ AN SAT READING PASSAGE

Some students find Critical Reading passages dull or intimidating. Remember that each passage is written for a purpose: The author wants to make a point, describe a situation, or convince you of his or her ideas. Sometimes, the little intro will tell you what the purpose is. Sometimes you must figure it out for yourself.

As you're reading, ask yourself, "What's the point of this? What's this all about?" This is active reading, and it's key to staying focused on the page. Active reading doesn't mean reading the passage word for word. It means reading lightly, but with a focus. Skim the passage, getting a general idea of what it's trying to get across.

———— ❖ ————

Read the passage quickly, with a focus on its general outline.

———— ❖ ————

Getting hung up on details is a major Critical Reading pitfall. You need to grasp the outline, but you don't need to get all the fine features. The questions will help you fill in the details by directing you back to important information in the passage.

HINT: *The less time you spend reading the passages, the more time you'll have to answer the questions — and that's where you score points.*

❑ TEST YOUR CRITICAL READING SMARTS

Test your reading skills on the following passage. Remember to read quickly and actively, going for the general outline of the piece. It's a difficult passage, but that doesn't mean you can't get points out of it.

In this essay, the author writes about her childhood on a Caribbean island that was an English colony for many years.

When I saw England for the first time, I was a child in school sitting at a desk. The England I was looking at was laid out on a map gently, beautifully, delicately, a very special jewel; it lay on a bed of sky blue, its
Line yellow form mysterious, because though it looked like a leg of mutton,*
(5) it could not really look like anything so familiar as a leg of mutton because it was England. England was a special jewel all right, and only special people got to wear it. The people who got to wear England were English people. They wore it well and they wore it everywhere: in jungles, in deserts, on plains, in places where they were not welcome, in
(10) places they should not have been. When my teacher had pinned this map up on the blackboard, she said, "This is England" — and she said it with authority, seriousness, and adoration, and we all sat up. We understood then — we were meant to understand then — that England was to be our source of myth and the source from which we got our sense of
(15) reality, our sense of what was meaningful, our sense of what was meaningless — and much about our own lives and much about the very idea of us headed that last list.

At the time I was a child sitting at my desk seeing England for the first time, I was already very familiar with the greatness of it. Each morn-
(20) ing before I left for school, I ate a breakfast of half a grapefruit, a bowl of oat porridge, bread and butter and a slice of cheese, and a cup of cocoa. The can of cocoa was often left on the table in front of me. It had written on it the name of the company, the year the company was established, and the words "Made in England." Those words, "Made in England,"
(25) were written on the box the oats came in too. The shoes I wore were made in England; so were my socks and cotton undergarments and the satin ribbons I wore tied at the end of two plaits of my hair. My father, who might have sat next to me at breakfast, was a carpenter and cabinet maker. The shoes he wore to work would have been made in England, as
(30) were his khaki shirt and trousers, his underpants and undershirt, his socks and brown felt hat. Felt was not the proper material from which a hat that was expected to provide shade from the hot sun should be made, but my father must have seen and admired a picture of an Englishman wearing such a hat in England. As we sat at breakfast a car might go by.
(35) The car, a Hillman or a Zephyr, was made in England. The very conception of the meal itself, breakfast, and its substantial quality and quantity was an idea from England; we somehow knew that in England they

began the day with this meal called breakfast and a proper breakfast was
a big breakfast.

(40)   At the time I saw this map — seeing England for the first time — I
did not say to myself, "Ah, so that's what it looks like," because there
was no longing in me to put a shape to those three words that ran
through every part of my life, no matter how small; for me to have had
such a longing would have meant that I lived in a certain atmosphere, an
(45) atmosphere in which those three words were felt as a burden. But I did
not live in such an atmosphere. My father's brown felt hat would devel-
op a hole in its crown, the lining would separate from the hat itself, and
six weeks before he thought that he could not be seen wearing it — he
was a very vain man — he would order another hat from England. And
(50) my mother taught me to eat my food in the English way: the knife in the
right hand, the fork in the left, my elbows held still close to my side.
When I had finally mastered it, I overheard her saying to a friend, "Did
you see how nicely she can eat?" But I knew then that I enjoyed my food
more when I ate it with my bare hands, and I continued to do so when
(55) she wasn't looking. And when my teacher showed us the map, she asked
us to study it carefully, because no test we would ever take would be
complete without this statement: "Draw a map of England."

      I did not know then that the statement "Draw a map of England"
was something far worse than a declaration of war. I did not know then
(60) that this statement was part of a process that would result in my erasure,
not my physical erasure, but my erasure all the same. I did not know
then that this statement was meant to make me feel in awe and small
whenever I heard the word "England": awe at its existence, small
because I was not from it. I did not know very much of anything then —
(65) certainly not what a blessing it was that I was unable to draw a map of
England correctly.

*the flesh of a sheep

How did you do? Yes, this was a tough passage. But you should
have gotten the general idea — that the author resents somewhat the
strong influence England had on every aspect of her childhood. As
the introduction told you, this island was "an English colony for many
years." It's clear throughout that the author rebels against her "erasure" — that is, the assumption that she and her country were
insignificant compared to mighty England. So that's all you really
need to take away from a quick reading of the passage. Remember:

Reading the passage won't earn you points — it's the questions that count.

❑ THE 5-STEP METHOD FOR CRITICAL READING QUESTIONS

Here's the Kaplan approach to Critical Reading questions:

1. READ THE QUESTION STEM
This is the place to really read carefully. Take a second to make sure you understand what the question is asking.

❖

Make sure you understand exactly what the question is looking for.

❖

2. LOCATE THE MATERIAL YOU NEED
If you are given a line reference, read the material surrounding the line mentioned. It will clarify exactly what the question is asking.

If you're not given a line reference, scan the text to find the place where the question applies, and reread those few sentences. Keep the main outline of the passage in mind.

❖

If a question has a specific line reference, always go back and reread the cited place in the passage.

❖

3. COME UP WITH AN IDEA OF THE RIGHT ANSWER
Don't spend time making up a precise answer. You need only a general sense of what you're after, so you can recognize the correct answer quickly when you see it.

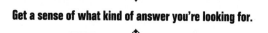

———— ❖ ————

Get a sense of what kind of answer you're looking for.

———— ❖ ————

4. SCAN THE ANSWER CHOICES

Quickly read the choices, looking for one that fits your idea of the right answer. If you don't find an ideal answer, quickly eliminate wrong choices by checking back to the passage. Rule out choices that are too extreme (the test makers rarely make outrageous statements, except in wrong answers) or that go against common sense. And get rid of answers that sound reasonable, but don't really answer the precise question asked.

———— ❖ ————

Rule out choices that are too extreme, that go against common sense, or that don't really answer the question.

———— ❖ ————

5. SELECT YOUR ANSWER

You've eliminated the obvious wrong answers. One of the few remaining should fit your ideal. If you're left with more than one contender, consider the passage's main idea, and make an educated guess.

———— ❖ ————

Use the Kaplan 5-Step Method for Critical Reading

———— ❖ ————

❏ APPLYING THE 5-STEP METHOD

Try the 5-Step Method on question 1 from the sample reading passage.

1. According to the author, England could not really look like a leg of mutton (line 5) because

   (A) maps generally don't give an accurate impression of what a place looks like

   (B) England was too grand and exotic a place for such a mundane image

   (C) England was an island not very different in appearance from her own island

   (D) the usual metaphor used to describe England was a precious jewel

   (E) mutton was one of the few foods familiar to her that did not come from England

1. READ THE QUESTION STEM

In this case, the question is straightforward: Why couldn't England really look like a leg of mutton? (Notice that "mutton" is defined for you at the end of the passage — you aren't expected to know the meaning of unfamiliar terms.)

2. LOCATE THE MATERIAL YOU NEED

You're given a clue: The answer lies somewhere near line 5. But don't read just that line — read the line or two before and after as well. By doing so, you learn that England was mysterious and special, so it couldn't look like something as familiar (to the author) as a leg of mutton.

3. COME UP WITH AN IDEA OF THE RIGHT ANSWER

After reading those couple of lines, you'd expect the answer to be something like "England was too special to look like a familiar leg of mutton."

4. SCAN THE ANSWER CHOICES

Choice (B) comes close to the ideal — it should have popped out. But if you weren't sure, you could have quickly eliminated the other choices. Thinking of the general thrust would have helped you eliminate (A) and (C). England was precious — like a jewel — but the author doesn't imply that England was usually compared to a jewel (D). And you never learn where mutton comes from (E).

❖

**Keep the general thrust of a passage in mind
when evaluating answer choices.**

❖

5. SELECT YOUR ANSWER

Choice (B) is the only one that works here. By reading the material that surrounds the line reference and putting an answer into your own words, you should have been able to choose (B) with confidence.

> HINT: From the questions, you can "fill in" the information you don't get in a quick reading. It's a way of working backward to reconstruct the passage.

❖

Use the questions to sharpen your understanding of the passage.

❖

Now try the 5-Step Method on the remaining questions for the sample passage.

2. The author's reference to felt as "not the proper material" (line 31) for her father's hat chiefly serves to emphasize her point about the
   (A) extremity of the local weather
   (B) arrogance of island laborers
   (C) informality of dress on the island
   (D) weakness of local industries
   (E) predominance of English culture

3. The word "conception" as used in line 35-36 means
   (A) beginning
   (B) image
   (C) origination
   (D) notion
   (E) plan

4. The word "erasure" (lines 60–61) as used by the author most nearly means
   (A) total annihilation
   (B) physical disappearance
   (C) sense of insignificance
   (D) enforced censorship
   (E) loss of freedom

5. The main purpose of the passage is to
   (A) advocate a change in the way a subject is taught in school
   (B) convey the personality of certain figures from the author's childhood
   (C) describe an overwhelming influence on the author's early life
   (D) analyze the importance of a sense of place to early education
   (E) relate a single formative episode in the author's life

6. For the author, the requirement to "Draw a map of England" (lines 55–66) represented an attempt to
   (A) force students to put their studies to practical use
   (B) glorify one culture at the expense of another
   (C) promote an understanding of world affairs
   (D) encourage students to value their own heritage
   (E) impart outmoded and inappropriate knowledge

We'll discuss the different types of Critical Reading questions in the next Step, Critical Reading Focused Techniques, where some of the questions above will be discussed further. For now, here are the credited answers:

1. (B)
2. (E)
3. (D)
4. (C)
5. (C)
6. (B)

Step 10 Recap: Reading Basic Techniques

The Important Tips From This Step

➤ Don't skip the brief introductions. They'll help you focus your reading.

➤ Read the passage quickly, with a focus on its general outline.

➤ Use the Kaplan 5-Step Method for Critical Reading:

1. Read the question stem.

2. Locate the material you need.

3. Get an idea of the answer.

4. Scan the answer choices.

5. Select your answer.

➤ Make sure you understand exactly what the question is looking for.

➤ If a question has a specific line reference always go back and reread the cited place in the passage.

➤ Get a sense of what kind of answer you're looking for.

➤ Rule out choices that are too extreme, that go against common sense, or that don't really answer the question.

➤ Keep the general thrust of the passage in mind when evaluating answer choices.

➤ Use the questions to sharpen your understanding of the passage.

Step 11: Critical Reading Focused Techniques

ALL CRITICAL READING QUESTIONS ARE NOT EQUAL

Most SAT Critical Reading questions fall into three basic types. Big Picture questions test your overall understanding of the passage's general outline. Little Picture questions ask about localized bits of information. Vocabulary-in-Context questions ask for the meaning of a single word.

In the sample passage in the previous step, question 5 is an example of a Big Picture question. Question 2 is an example of a Little Picture question. Question 3 is a Vocabulary-in-Context question.

> HINT: *Remember to skip around if you need to. You can tackle whichever passage you like in any order you like within the same section. But once you've read through the passage, try all the questions that go with it.*

❏ BIG PICTURE QUESTIONS

Big Picture questions test your overall understanding of a passage. They might ask about:

➤ the main point or purpose of a passage

➤ the author's attitude or tone

➤ the logic underlying the author's argument

➤ how ideas relate to each other

One way to see the Big Picture is to read actively. As you read, ask yourself, "What's this all about? What's the point of this? Why is the author saying this?"

HINT: Still stumped after reading the passage? Do the Little Picture questions first. They can help you fill in the Big Picture.

Turn back to the passage you tried in the previous step. What did you get out of the first reading? Something like "England was a profound influence on the author's early life, and she resents that"? That would have been enough.

Now look at question 5. It's a Big Picture question, asking for the main point of the passage. Use the 5-Step Method to find your answer.

5. The main purpose of the passage is to
  (A) advocate a change in the way a subject is taught in school
  (B) convey the personality of certain figures from the author's childhood
  (C) describe an overwhelming influence on the author's early life
  (D) analyze the importance of a sense of place to early education
  (E) relate a single formative episode in the author's life

1. READ THE QUESTION STEM
Simple enough: What's the main point of the passage?

2. LOCATE THE MATERIAL YOU NEED
In this case, you're asked about the overall point. You should have gotten a sense of that from reading the passage.

3. GET AN IDEA OF THE RIGHT ANSWER
Again, you just need a rough statement. Here, something like this would do: "The purpose is to describe how England was a huge influence, and how the author resented that."

4. SCAN THE ANSWER CHOICES

(C) should have popped out. But (D) might also have looked good if you focused on the words "sense of place." So put those two aside as contenders. (A), how a subject was taught in school, is too narrow, and the same goes for (B), figures in the author's childhood, and (E), a single formative episode.

5. SELECT YOUR ANSWER

You've crossed off the poor choices, and you're down to two possibilities. Which matches your ideal? (C) comes closer. Look closely at (D) and you'll see that it's too general, too impersonal. Go with the best choice.

———————— ❖ ————————

Do Big Picture Questions after Little Picture Questions if you're not clear on the main idea of the passage.

———————— ❖ ————————

❑ LITTLE PICTURE QUESTIONS

More than two thirds of Critical Reading questions ask about Little Pictures. Little Picture questions usually refer you to a particular line or paragraph. That's a strong clue to where in the passage you'll find your answer.

Little Picture questions might:

➤ test whether you understand significant information that's stated in the passage

➤ ask you to make inferences or draw conclusions based on a part of the passage

➤ ask you to relate parts of the passage to one another

Question 2 is a Little Picture question:

2. The author's reference to felt as "not the proper material" (line 31) for her father's hat chiefly serves to emphasize her point about the
   (A) extremity of the local weather
   (B) arrogance of island laborers
   (C) informality of dress on the island
   (D) weakness of local industries
   (E) predominance of English culture

You're asked about the felt hat of the author's father; what does this point emphasize? Applying Kaplan's Step 2, locate the material you'll need. You're given a clue — a line reference — to help you here. Reread that, and the lines before and after it as well.

> HINT: Don't pick farfetched inferences. SAT inferences tend to be strongly implied in the passage.

So why did the father wear a felt hat, which was probably quite hot in the tropical sun? Because it was English. That's what correct choice (E) says. Rereading that bit of the passage should have led you straight to that answer. (A) comes close, but doesn't fit the general thrust of the passage, which has little to do with describing the local weather but a lot to do with the overpowering influence of England. Even with Little Picture questions, grasping the general thrust of the passage can help you find the correct answer.

— ❖ —

Make sure your answer to a Little Picture question makes sense in the context of the passage.

— ❖ —

❑ VOCABULARY-IN-CONTEXT

Vocabulary-in-Context questions ask about an even smaller part of the passage than other Little Picture questions do; they ask about the usage of a single word. These questions do not test your ability to define hard words like "archipelago" and "garrulous." They do test your ability to infer the meaning of a word from context.

The words tested in these questions may be familiar to you; often they are fairly common words with more than one definition. Many of the answer choices will be definitions of the tested word, but only one will work in context. Vocabulary-in-Context questions always have a line reference, and you should always use it!

> HINT: Context *is the most important part of Vocabulary-in-Context questions.*

Sometimes one of the answer choices will jump out at you. It'll be the most common meaning of the word in question — but it's rarely right! We call this the "obvious" choice. For example, say "curious" is the word being tested. The obvious choice is "inquisitive." But "curious" also means "odd," and that's more likely to be the answer. Using context to find the answer will help prevent you from falling for this trap. You can use these choices to your advantage, though: If you get stuck on a Vocabulary-in-Context question, you can eliminate the "obvious" choice and take a guess instead.

❖

If a Vocabulary-in-Context question has an "obvious" choice, be wary of it.

❖

VOCABULARY-IN-CONTEXT PRACTICE

Here's some practice with Vocabulary-in-Context questions. Remember, don't just pick a common definition of the word in question. Pick the choice that defines what it means in context.

1. Embodied and given life in the social realities of her own period, Jane Austen's satire still has currency in ours.

   In the lines above, "currency" most nearly means
   (A) usualness
   (B) stylishness
   (C) prevalence
   (D) funds
   (E) relevance

2. Captain Wentworth had no fortune. He had been lucky in his profession, but, spending freely what had come freely, had realized nothing.

   Which most nearly captures the meaning of the word "realized" in the sentence above?
   (A) understood
   (B) accomplished
   (C) learned
   (D) accumulated
   (E) fulfilled

3. Anyone with more than a superficial knowledge of Shakespeare's plays must necessarily entertain some doubt concerning their true authorship.

In the lines above, "entertain" most nearly means

(A) amuse

(B) harbor

(C) occupy

(D) cherish

(E) engage

Answers

1. (E)
2. (D)
3. (B)

❏ PAIRED PASSAGES — A (NOT SO) SPECIAL CASE

Don't let the paired passages worry you — they're not twice as hard as the single reading selections. With paired passages, focus as you read on the relationship between the two passages. Just as with single passages, the questions following paired passages can help fill in the picture.

IMPORTANT: Questions following paired passages are also ordered. The first few questions relate to the first passage, the next few to the second passage, and the final questions ask about how the passages relate.

HOW TO DO PAIRED PASSAGES

1. Skim the first passage, looking for the general outline (as you would with a single passage).
2. Do the questions that relate to the first passage.
3. Skim the second passage, looking for the general outline and thinking about how the second passage relates to the first.
4. Do the questions that relate to the second passage.
5. Now you're ready to do the remaining questions, which will ask about the relationship between the two passages.

Alternating skimming passages and answering questions is especially important if you're short of time. You'll be able to answer at least some of the questions (and get a few extra points) before time runs out. By the time you've looked at both passages and answered the questions about each passage, you'll have a firm sense of the relationship between the pair. That will help you to answer the last group of questions.

❖
Take the paired passages one at a time.
❖

❏ SPECIAL TIMING ADVICE

WHAT TO DO IF YOU RUN OUT OF TIME

It's always best to skim the passage before you hit the questions. But if you only have a few minutes left, here's how to score points even while time is running out.

You can answer Vocabulary-in-Context questions and many Little Picture questions without reading the passage. If the question has a line reference, locate the material you need to find your answer and follow the 5-Step Method as usual. You won't have the overall picture to guide you, but you might be able to reach the correct answer just by understanding the "Little Picture."

❖
If you're running out of time, skip reading a passage and just do its Vocabulary-in-Context questions first, then its Little Picture questions.
❖

CRITICAL READING POP QUIZ

7 questions
10 minutes

Questions 1–7 are based on the following passage

The following excerpt is from a speech delivered in 1873 by Susan B. Anthony, a leader in the women's rights movement of the 19th century.

Friends and fellow-citizens: I stand before you tonight under indictment for the alleged crime of having voted at the last Presidential election, without having a lawful right to vote. It shall be my work this
(Line)
(5) evening to prove to you that in thus voting, I not only committed no crime, but, instead, simply exercised my citizen's rights, guaranteed to me and all United States citizens by the National Constitution, beyond the power of any State to deny.

The preamble of the Federal Constitution says:
(10) "We, the people of the United States, in order to form a more perfect union, establish justice, insure domestic tranquillity, provide for the common defense, promote the general welfare, and secure the blessings of liberty to ourselves and our posterity, do ordain and establish this Constitution for the United States of America."

(15) It was we, the people; not we, the white male citizens; nor yet we, the male citizens; but we, the whole people, who formed the Union. And we formed it, not to give the blessings of liberty, but to secure them; not to the half of ourselves and the half of our posterity, but to the whole people — women as well as men. And it is a downright mockery to talk to women of their enjoyment of the blessings of liberty while they are
(20) denied the use of the only means of securing them provided by this democratic-republican government — the ballot.

For any State to make sex a qualification that must ever result in the disfranchisement* of one entire half of the people is a violation of the supreme law of the land. By it the blessings of liberty are forever with-
(25) held from women and their female posterity. To them this government had no just powers derived from the consent of the governed. To them this government is not a democracy. It is not a republic. It is an odious aristocracy; a hateful oligarchy of sex; this oligarchy of sex, which makes father, brothers, husband, sons, the oligarchs over the mother and sis-
(30) ters, the wife and daughters of every household — which ordains all men

sovereigns, all women subjects, carries dissension, discord and rebellion into every home of the nation.

Webster, Worcester and Bouvier all define a citizen to be a person in the United States, entitled to vote and hold office.

(35) The one question left to be settled now is: Are women persons? And I hardly believe any of our opponents will have the hardihood to say they are not. Being persons, then, women are citizens; and no State has a right to make any law, or to enforce any old law, that shall abridge their privileges or immunities. Hence, every discrimination against women in (40) the constitutions and laws of the several States is today null and void, precisely as is every one against Negroes.

*disfranchisement: deprivation of the right to vote.

1. In the first paragraph, Anthony states that her action in voting was
   (A) illegal, but morally justified
   (B) the result of her keen interest in national politics
   (C) legal, if the Constitution is interpreted correctly
   (D) an illustration of the need for a women's rights movement
   (E) illegal, but worthy of leniency

2. By saying "we, the people...the whole people, who formed the Union" (lines 9–15), Anthony means that
   (A) the founders of the nation conspired to deprive women of their rights
   (B) some male citizens are still being denied basic rights
   (C) the role of women in the founding of the nation is generally ignored
   (D) society is endangered when women are deprived of basic rights
   (E) all people deserve to enjoy the rights guaranteed by the Constitution

3. In the fifth paragraph, (lines 22–32), Anthony's argument rests mainly on the strategy of convincing her audience that

   (A) any state that denies women the vote undermines its status as a democracy

   (B) women deprived of the vote will eventually raise a rebellion

   (C) the nation will remain an aristocracy if the status of women does not change

   (D) women's rights issues should be debated in every home

   (E) even an aristocracy cannot survive without the consent of the governed

4. The word "hardihood" in (line 36) could best be replaced by

   (A) endurance

   (B) vitality

   (C) nerve

   (D) opportunity

   (E) stupidity

5. When Anthony warns that "no State...shall abridge their privileges" (line 37–39), she means that

   (A) women should be allowed to live a life of privilege

   (B) women on trial cannot be forced to give up their immunity

   (C) every state should repeal its outdated laws

   (D) governments may not deprive citizens of their rights

   (E) the rights granted to women must be decided by the people, not the state

EXPLANATIONS

1. (C)

This question is keyed to paragraph 1, where the second sentence gives you Anthony's declaration that she "not only committed no crime, but...simply exercised my citizen's rights, guaranteed me...by the National Constitution." Her act, in other words, was legal according to her reading of the Constitution. So (C) is correct.

2. (E)

Anthony points out here that no subgroup was excluded by the wording of the Constitution's "we, the people" preamble. That preamble refers "not to the half of ourselves...but to...women as well as men." So (E) is the best answer. (D) may have appealed to you, but it's wrong since it describes a claim that Anthony doesn't make until the following paragraph (note those line references!).

3. (A)

In the paragraph referred to, Anthony says that any state that prohibits women from voting violates federal law — the Constitution. A state that does so becomes "an odious aristocracy, a hateful oligarchy." In other words, a state that denies women the vote can't legitimately call itself either a democracy or a republic, so (A) is the best restatement of this rather subtle inference.

4. (C)

"Hardihood" is a strange word, but its meaning is clear in the keyed sentence. Anthony says, essentially, that her opponents wouldn't "have the hardihood" to claim that women are not persons. These opponents wouldn't, in other words, have the "nerve" to do so, choice (C). (Treat this like a Sentence Completion: Look for a word that could replace "hardihood" in the sentence; don't just look for any acceptable definition of "hardihood.")

5. (D)
To abridge means to curtail or decrease in some way, so Anthony is arguing here that, since women are citizens, no state can curtail or decrease or deprive them of their rights. (D) is therefore the best answer.

Step 11 Recap: Reading Focused Techniques

The Important Tips From This Step

➤ Do Big Picture questions after Little Picture questions if you're not clear on the main idea of the passage.

➤ Make sure your answer to a Little Picture question makes sense in the context of the passage.

➤ If a Vocabulary-in-Context question has an "obvious" choice, be wary of it.

➤ Take the paired passages one at at time.

➤ If you're running out of time, skip reading a passage and do its Vocabulary-in-Context questions first, then its Little Picture questions.

Avoiding Those Dreaded Math Traps

✔ At-a-Glance

Below are the topics covered in today's lesson. Check each topic as you complete it. If you have time later, come back to any topics you've skipped or not understood entirely.

STEP 12 — MATH TRAP TECHNIQUES

❏ How Math Traps Work and How to Avoid Them

The Top Traps
❏ Percent Increase/Decrease
❏ Weighted Averages
❏ Ratio:Ratio:Ratio
❏ Unspecified Order
❏ Length:Area Ratio
❏ Hidden Instructions
❏ Average Rate
❏ Counting Numbers
(Time: 120 minutes)

Step 12: Math Trap Techniques

LOOK BEFORE YOU LEAP

It's time for us to let you in on a little secret that will allow you to breeze through the entire SAT, get into any college you want, succeed in life, and find eternal happiness.

If you believed a word of the preceding sentence, you need to pay special attention to this chapter. This step presents eight common SAT traps. Traps lure you into one answer, usually an answer that's easy to get to. But they conceal the correct answer, which requires some thought. If you're not wary of traps on the SAT, they may trip you up. Learn to recognize common traps and you'll gain more points on test day.

❑ HOW MATH TRAPS WORK AND HOW TO AVOID THEM

The same traps occur again and again on the SAT. You can boost your score by learning how they work and how to avoid them. Once you can deal with traps, you'll do much better on the harder math questions.

---- ❖ ----

**If you see what appears to be an easy problem late in a
question set, there is probably a trap.**

---- ❖ ----

Let's look at the eight most common math traps on the SAT:

❏ TRAP #1: PERCENT INCREASE/DECREASE

EXAMPLE

Jackie purchased a new car in 1990. Three years later she sold it to a dealer for 40 percent less than she paid for it in 1990. The dealer then added 20 percent onto the price he paid and resold it to another customer. The price the final customer paid for the car was what percent of the original price Jackie paid in 1990?

(A) 40%

(B) 60%

(C) 72%

(D) 80%

(E) 88%

THE WRONG ANSWER

The increase/decrease percentage problem usually appears at the end of a section and invariably contains a trap. Most students will figure that taking away 40 percent, and then adding 20 percent gives you an overall loss of 20 percent, and pick choice (D), 80 percent, as the correct answer. Wrong!

THE TRAP

When a quantity is increased or decreased by a percentage more than once, you cannot simply add and subtract the percents to get the answer.

In this kind of percent problem:

➤ The first percent change is a percent of the starting amount, but the second change is a percent of the *new* amount.

AVOIDING THE TRAP

Percents can only be added and subtracted when they are percents of the same amount.

Don't blindly add and subtract percents.

FINDING THE RIGHT ANSWER

We know:

➤ the "40 percent less" that Jackie got for the car is 40 percent of her original price

➤ the 20 percent the dealer adds on is 20 percent of what the dealer paid, a much smaller amount

➤ adding on 20 percent of that smaller amount is not the same thing as adding back 20 percent of the original price

SOLVING THE PROBLEM FAST

Use 100 for a starting quantity, whether or not it's plausible in the real situation. The problem asks for the relative amount of change. So you can take any starting number, and compare it with the final result. Because you're dealing with percents, 100 is the easiest number to work with.

HINT: *Pick 100 as the starting quantity.*

➤ If Jackie paid $100 for the car, what is 40 percent less?

In the case of $100, each percent equals $1, so 100 − 40 = 60. Jackie sold the car for $60.

➤ If the dealer charges 20 percent more than his purchase price, he's raising the price by 20 percent of $60, which is $60 × .20 = $12 (not 20 percent of $100, which would be $20!).

➤ Therefore the dealer sold the car again for $60 + $12, or $72.

➤ Finally, what percent of the starting price ($100) is $72? $\frac{72}{100}$ = 72%. So the correct answer here is choice (C).

❑ TRAP #2: WEIGHTED AVERAGES

EXAMPLE

In a class of 27 students, the average (arithmetic mean) score of the boys on the final exam was 83. If the average score of the 15 girls in the class was 92, what was the average of the whole class?

(A) 86.2

(B) 87.0

(C) 87.5

(D) 88.0

(E) 88.2

THE WRONG ANSWER

Some students will rush in and simply average 83 and 92 to come up with 87.5 as the class average.

THE TRAP

You cannot combine averages of different quantities by taking the average of those averages.

In an averages problem, if one value occurs more frequently than others it is "weighted" more. Remember that the average formula calls for the sum of all the terms, divided by the total number of terms.

AVOIDING THE TRAP

Work with the sums, not the averages.

Don't just take the average of the averages.

FINDING THE RIGHT ANSWER

If 15 of the 27 students are girls, the remaining 12 must be boys.

We can't just add 83 to 92 and divide by two. In this class there are more girls than boys, and therefore the girls' test scores are "weighted" more — they contribute more to the class average. So the answer must be either (D) or (E). To find each sum, multiply each average by the number of terms it represents. After you have found the sums of the different terms, find the combined average by plugging them into the average formula.

$$\text{Total class average} = \frac{\text{Sum of girls' scores + Sum of boys' scores}}{\text{Total number of students}}$$

$$= \frac{(\text{\# of girls} \times \text{girls' average score}) + (\text{\# of boys} \times \text{boys' average score})}{\text{Total number of students}}$$

$$= \frac{15(92) + 12(83)}{27} = \frac{1380 + 996}{27} = 88$$

So the class average is 88, answer choice (D). (Notice how using a calculator helps in this situation!)

☐ TRAP #3: RATIO:RATIO:RATIO

EXAMPLE

Mike's coin collection consists of quarters, dimes, and nickels. If the ratio of the number of quarters to the number of dimes is 5 to 2, and the ratio of the number of dimes to the number of nickels is 3 to 4, what is the ratio of the number of quarters to the number of nickels?

(A) 5 to 4

(B) 7 to 5

(C) 10 to 6

(D 12 to 7

(E) 15 to 8

THE WRONG ANSWER

If you chose 5 to 4 as the correct answer, you fell for the classic ratio trap.

THE TRAP

Parts of different ratios don't always refer to the same whole.

In the classic ratio trap, two different ratios each share a common part that is represented by two different numbers. The two ratios do not refer to the same whole, however, so they are not in proportion to each other. To solve this type of problem, restate both ratios so that the numbers representing the common part (in this case "dimes") are the same. Then all the parts will be in proportion and can be compared to each other.

AVOIDING THE TRAP

Make sure the common quantity in both ratios has the same number in both.

❖

Restate ratios so that the same number refers to the same quantity.

❖

FINDING THE RIGHT ANSWER

To find the ratio of quarters to nickels, restate both ratios so that the number of dimes is the same in both.

We are given two ratios:

Quarters to Dimes = 5 to 2   Dimes to Nickels = 3 to 4

The number corresponding to dimes in the first ratio is 2.
The number corresponding to dimes in the second ratio is 3.
To restate the ratios, find the least common multiple of 2 and 3.
The least common multiple of 2 and 3 is 2 × 3, or 6.

Restate the ratios with the number of dimes as 6:

Quarters to Dimes = 15 to 6 (which is the same as 5 to 2)
Dimes to Nickels = 6 to 8 (which is the same as 3 to 4)

The ratios are still in their original proportions, but now they can be compared easily, since dimes are represented by the same number in both.

The ratio of quarters to dimes to nickels is 15 to 6 to 8, so the ratio of quarters to nickels is 15 to 8, which is answer choice (E).

☐ TRAP #4: UNSPECIFIED ORDER

EXAMPLE

Column A   Column B

A, *B*, and *C* are points on a line such that point *A* is 12 units away from point *B* and point *B* is 4 units away from point *C*.

The distance from   16
point *A* to point *C*

THE WRONG ANSWER

In problems about distances on a line, you should always draw a diagram to help you visualize the relationship between the points.

In this diagram, the distance from A to C is 16, which is the same as Column B. But choice (C) is not the right answer.

THE TRAP

Don't assume that there is only one possible arrangement of the points. In this case, there's no reason to believe that the points lie in alphabetical order.

We are not told what the relationship between A and C is. In fact, C could lie to the left of B, like this:

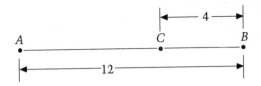

AVOIDING THE TRAP

Don't assume points lie in the order they are given or in alphabetical order — look for alternatives. In general:

Don't assume that information is given in the most useful or most logical order.

FINDING THE RIGHT ANSWER

In this second case, the distance from A to C is 8, which is less than Column B. Since we have two possible relationships between the columns, the answer must be (D) — you can't be certain from the data given.

❑ TRAP #5: LENGTH:AREA RATIO

EXAMPLE

Column A

The area of a square with
a perimeter of 14

Column B

Twice the area of a
square with a perimeter
of 7

THE WRONG ANSWER

Twice the perimeter doesn't mean twice the area. Choice (C) is
wrong.

THE TRAP

In proportional figures, the ratio of the areas is not the same as the
ratio of the lengths.

AVOIDING THE TRAP

Understand that the ratio of the areas of proportional figures is the
square of the ratio of corresponding linear measures.

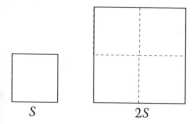

S

$2S$

❖

**Remember that, in proportional figures, the ratio of areas
is not the same as the ratio of lengths.**

❖

FINDING THE RIGHT ANSWER

One way to solve this QC would be to actually compute the respective areas.

A square of perimeter 14 has side length $\frac{14}{4}$ = 3.5. Its area then is $(3.5)^2$ = 12.25. On the other hand, the area of the square in Column B is $(\frac{7}{4})^2$ = $(1.75)^2$ = 3.0625. Even twice that area is still less than the 12.25 in Column A. The answer is (A).

But this method takes too much time. A quicker and cleverer way to dodge this trap is to understand the relationship between the linear ratio and the area ratio of proportional figures. In proportional figures, the area ratio is the square of the linear ratio.

In the example above, we are given two squares with sides in a ratio of 14:7 or 2:1.

Using the rule above, we square the linear 2:1 ratio. The areas of the two figures will be in a 4:1 ratio.

The same goes for circles:

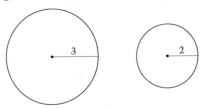

In the figure above, we are given two circles with radii in a 3:2 ratio. Using the rule above, we square the linear 3:2 ratio to get $3^2:2^2$, or 9:4. The areas of the two circles will be in a 9:4 ratio.

❑ TRAP #6: HIDDEN INSTRUCTIONS

EXAMPLE

At a certain restaurant, the hourly wage for a waiter is 20 percent greater than the hourly wage for a dishwasher, and the hourly wage for a dishwasher is half as much as the hourly wage for a cook's assistant. If a cook's assistant earns $8.50 an hour, how much less than a cook's assistant does a waiter earn each hour?

(A) $2.55

(B) $3.40

(C) $4.25

(D) $5.10

(E) $5.95

THE WRONG ANSWER

To solve this problem, you must find the hourly wage of the waiter.

The cook's assistant earns $8.50 an hour.

The dishwasher earns half that, or $4.25 an hour

The waiter earns 20 percent more than this: $4.25 × 1.2 = $5.10.

So the waiter earns $5.10 an hour, and you might reach automatically to fill in answer choice (D). But (D) is the wrong answer.

THE TRAP

A small step, easily overlooked, can mean the difference between a right and wrong answer.

In this case the word is "less." After spending all this time finding the waiter's hourly wage, many students skip right over the vital last step. They overlook the fact that the question asks not what the waiter earns, but how much less than the cook's assistant the waiter earns.

AVOIDING THE TRAP

Make sure you answer the question that's being asked.

Watch for hidden instructions.

FINDING THE RIGHT ANSWER

You have figured out that the waiter earns $5.10 an hour.

And the cook's assistant earns $8.50 an hour.

To find out how much less than the cook's assistant the waiter earns, subtract the waiter's hourly wage from the cook's assistant's hourly wage.

The correct answer is (B), $3.40.

❏ TRAP #7. AVERAGE RATE

EXAMPLE

A car traveled from A to B at an average rate of 40 miles per hour and then immediately traveled back from B to A at an average speed of 60 miles per hour. What was the car's average speed for the round trip, in miles per hour?

(A) 45

(B) 48

(C) 50

(D) 52

(E) 54

THE WRONG ANSWER

Do you see which answer choice is too "obvious" to be correct? The temptation is simply to average 40 and 60. The answer is "obviously" (C), 50. But 50 is wrong.

THE TRAP

To get an average rate, you can't just average the rates.

Why is the average speed not 50 mph? Because the car spent more time traveling at 40 mph than at 60 mph. Each leg of the round trip was the same distance, but the first leg, at the slower speed, took more time.

AVOIDING THE TRAP

You can solve almost any Average Rate problem with this general formula:

$$\text{Average Rate} = \frac{\text{Total Distance}}{\text{Total Time}}$$

Use the given information to figure out the Total Distance and the Total Time. But how can you do that when many problems don't specify the distances?

FINDING THE RIGHT ANSWER

In our sample above, we are told that a car went "from A to B at 40 miles per hour and back from B to A at 60 miles per hour."

In other words, it went half the Total Distance at 40 mph and half the Total Distance at 60 mph.

How do you use the formula, Average Rate = $\frac{\text{Total Distance}}{\text{Total Time}}$, if you don't know the Total Distance?

> HINT: *Pick any number you want for the Total Distance. Pick a useful number!*

Divide that Total Distance into Half Distances.

Calculate the time needed to travel each Half Distance at the different rates.

---------- ❖ ----------

When plugging numbers into the Average Rate formula, pick numbers that are easy to work with.

---------- ❖ ----------

A good number to pick here would be 240 miles for the Total Distance, because you can easily figure in your head the times for two 120-mile legs at 40 mph and 60 mph:

A to B: $\frac{120 \text{ miles}}{40 \text{ miles per hour}} = 3$ hours

B to A: $\frac{120 \text{ miles}}{60 \text{ miles per hour}} = 2$ hours

Total Time = 5 hours

Now plug "Total Distance = 240 miles" and "Total Time = 5 hours" into the general formula:

Average Rate = $\dfrac{\text{Total Distance}}{\text{Total Time}}$

$\quad\quad\quad = \dfrac{240 \text{ miles}}{5 \text{ hours}}$

$\quad\quad\quad = 48$ miles per hour.

Correct answer choice: (B).

❏ TRAP #8: COUNTING NUMBERS

EXAMPLE

The tickets for a certain raffle are consecutively numbered.
If Louis sold the tickets numbered from 75 to 148 inclusive,
how many raffle tickets did he sell?

(Note: This is a Grid-in, so there are no choices.)

THE WRONG ANSWER

Many people would subtract 75 from 148 to get 73 as their answer.
But that is not correct.

THE TRAP

Subtracting the first and last integers in a range will give you the difference of the two numbers. It won't give you the number of integers in that range.

AVOIDING THE TRAP

To count the number of integers in a range, subtract the endpoints and then add 1.

If you forget the rule, pick two small numbers that are close together, such as 1 and 4. Obviously, there are four integers from 1 to 4, inclusive. But if you had subtracted 1 from 4, you would have gotten 3. In the diagram below, you can see that 3 is actually the distance between the integers, if the integers were on a number line or a ruler.

❖

To count the number of integers in a range, subtract the endpoints and then add 1.

❖

FINDING THE RIGHT ANSWER

In the problem above, subtract 75 from 148.

The result is 73.

Add 1 to this difference to get the number of integers.

That gives you 74. This is the number you would grid in on your answer sheet.

The word "inclusive" tells you to include the first and last numbers given. So "the integers from 5 to 15 inclusive" *include* 5 and 15. Questions always make it clear whether you should include the outer numbers or not, since the correct answer hinges on this point.

13 questions
10 minutes

Column A   Column B

A car traveled the first half of a 100-kilometer distance at an average speed of 120 kilometers per hour and it traveled the remaining distance at an average speed of 80 kilometers per hour.

1. The car's average speed   100
   in kilometers per hour, for
   the 100 kilometers

The ratio of $\frac{1}{4}$ to $\frac{2}{5}$ is equal to the ratio of $\frac{2}{5}$ to x.

2. x $\frac{3}{5}$

John buys 34 books at $6 each, and 17 at $12 each.

3. The average price John $9.00
   pays per book

On a certain highway, Town X lies 50 miles away from Town Y, and Town Z lies 80 miles from Town X.

4. The number of minutes a   30
   car traveling at
   an average speed of 60 miles
   per hour takes to travel from
   Town Y to Town Z

Column A	Column B

5. The area of a circle with a diameter of 3

The sum of the areas of 3 circles each with a diameter of 1

Jane invests her savings in a fund that adds 10 percent interest to her savings at the end of every year.

6. The percent by which her money has increased after 3 years

31 percent

---

7. Pump 1 can drain a 400-gallon water tank in 1.2 hours. Pump 2 can drain the same tank in 1.8 hours. How many minutes longer than pump 1 would it take pump 2 to drain a 100-gallon tank?

   (A) 0.15
   (B) 1.2
   (C) 6
   (D) 9
   (E) 18

8. Volumes 12 through 30 of a certain encyclopedia are located on the bottom shelf of a bookcase. If the volumes of the encyclopedia are numbered consecutively, how many volumes of the encyclopedia are on the bottom shelf?

(A) 17
(B) 18
(C) 19
(D) 29
(E) 30

9. A reservoir is at full capacity at the beginning of summer. By the first day of fall, the level in the reservoir is 30 percent below full capacity. Then during the fall a period of heavy rains raises the level by 30 percent. After the rains, the reservoir is at what percent of its full capacity?

(A) 100%
(B) 95%
(C) 91%
(D) 85%
(E) 60%

10. Two classes, one with 50 students, the other with 30, take the same exam. The combined average of both classes is 84.5. If the larger class averages 80, what is the average of the smaller class?

(A) 87.2
(B) 89.0
(C) 92.0
(D) 93.3
(E) 94.5

11. In a pet shop, the ratio of puppies to kittens is 7:6 and the ratio of kittens to guinea pigs is 5:3. What is the ratio of puppies to guinea pigs?

    (A)   7:3
    (B)   6:5
    (C)   13:8
    (D)   21:11
    (E)   35:18

---

12. A typist typed the first n pages of a book, where n > 0, at an average rate of 12 pages per hour and typed the remaining n pages at an average rate of 20 pages per hour. What was the typist's average rate, in pages per hour, for the entire book?

    (A) $14\frac{2}{3}$

    (B)   15

    (C)   16

    (D)   17

    (E)   18

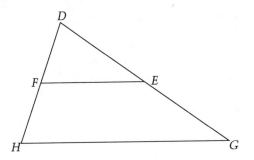

13. In triangle *DGH* above, *DE* = *EG*, *EF* || *GH*, and the area of triangle *DGH* is 30. What is the area of triangle *DEF*?

(This is a Grid-in question.)

ANSWERS

How did you do? Did you spot the trap in each problem? Use the answers below to see what your weaknesses are. Each wrong answer represents one trap you need to work on. Go back and reread the section on that trap. Then try the problems again, until you answer right.

1. (B) Average rates trap (see page 160)
2. (A) A variation on the Ratio:Ratio:Ratio trap — (see page 152)
3. (B) Weighted averages trap (see page 150)
4. (D) Unspecified order trap (see page 154)
5. (A) Length:area ratio trap (see page 156)
6. (A) Percent increase/decrease trap (see page 147)
7. (D) Hidden instructions trap (see page 158)
8. (C) Counting numbers trap (see page 163)
9. (C) Percent increase/decrease trap (see page 147)
10. (C) Weighted averages trap (see page 150)
11. (E) Ratio:ratio:ratio trap (see page 152)
12. (B) Average rates trap (see page 160)
13. 7.5 Length:area ratio trap (see page 156)

Step 12 Recap: Math Trap Techniques

The Important Tips From This Step

➤ If you see what appears to be an easy problem late in a question set, there is probably a trap.

➤ Don't blindly add and subtract percents.

➤ Don't just take the averages of averages.

➤ Restate ratios so that the same number refers to the same quantity.

➤ Don't assume that information is given in the most useful or logical order.

➤ Remember that, in proportional figures, the ratio of the areas is not the same as the ratio of the lengths.

➤ Watch for hidden instructions.

➤ When plugging numbers into the Average Rate formula, pick numbers that are easy to work with.

➤ To count the numbers of integers in a range, subtract the endpoints and then add 1.

Putting It All Together On Test Day

THE STEPS

✔ At-a-Glance

Below are the topics covered in today's lesson. Check each topic as you complete it. If you have time later, come back to any topics you've skipped or not understood entirely.

STEP 13 — GRID-IN TECHNIQUES

❑ The Format
❑ Filling in the Grid
❑ Grid-in Practice
(Time: 30 minutes)

STEP 14 — END-OF-TIME TECHNIQUES

❑ Eliminating Unreasonable Choices
❑ Eliminating the Obvious on Hard Questions
❑ Eyeballing Lengths, Angles, and Areas
❑ Finding the Range and Guessing on Grid-ins
❑ Looking for the Fast Points in Critical Reading
(Time: 30 minutes)

STEP 15 — LAST-MINUTE TIPS

☐ Three Days Before the Test
☐ Two Days Before the Test
☐ The Night Before the Test
☐ The Morning of the Test
☐ During the Test
☐ After the Test
☐ Post-SAT Festivities

(Time: 30 minutes)

Step 13: Grid-in Techniques

NOT YOUR AVERAGE SAT QUESTION

In high school math class, you usually don't get five answer choices to pick from on a test. And you don't lose a quarter of a point for a wrong answer. Instead, you are given a problem and you're asked to find the answer.

The Grid-in section on the SAT is a lot like the math tests you're already used to taking. Unlike other SAT Math questions, Grid-ins have no multiple-choice answers and there's no penalty for wrong answers. You have to figure out your own answer and fill it in on a special grid. Note that some Grid-ins have only one correct answer, while others have several correct credited answers, or even a range of such answers.

STATISTIC: *The 10 Grid-ins count for one-sixth of your Math score.*

10 Grid-In
Questions

❏ THE FORMAT

You'll get 10 Grid-ins, following the QCs, in one of the Math sections. Here's what the directions will look like:

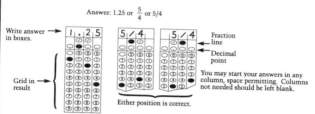

For each of the questions below (16-25), solve the problem and indicate your answer by darkening the ovals in the special grid. For example:

Answer: 1.25 or $\frac{5}{4}$ or 5/4

Write answer in boxes.

Grid in result

Either position is correct.

Fraction line

Decimal point

You may start your answers in any column, space permitting. Columns not needed should be left blank.

- It is recommended, though not required, that you write your answer in the boxes at the top of the columns. However, you will receive credit only for darkening the ovals correctly.

- Grid only one answer to a question, even though some problems have more than one correct answer.

- Darken no more than one oval in a column.

- No answers are negative.

- Mixed numbers cannot be gridded. For example: the number $1\frac{1}{4}$ must be gridded as 1.25 or 5/4.

  (If  is gridded, it will be interpreted as $\frac{11}{4}$ not $1\frac{1}{4}$.)

- Decimal Accuracy: Decimal answers must be entered as accurately as possible. For example, if you obtain an answer such as 0.1666..., you should record the result as .166 or .167. **Less accurate values such as .16 or .17 are not acceptable.**

  Acceptable ways to grid $\frac{1}{6}$ = .1666...

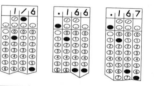

For each question, you'll see a grid with four boxes and a column of ovals, or "bubbles," beneath each. First write your numerical answer in the boxes, one digit, decimal point, or fraction sign per box. But the numbers in these boxes are there just to help you grid in properly. They're not read by the scoring computer.

———————— ❖ ————————

You can only get a point if you correctly fill in the ovals below the boxes.

———————— ❖ ————————

WARNING:

➤ Fill in no more than one oval per column.

➤ Make the oval you grid match your number above.

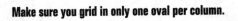
❏ FILLING IN THE GRID

The grid cannot accommodate
 ➤ negative answers
 ➤ answers with variables (x, y, w, etc.)
 ➤ answers greater than 9999
 ➤ answers with commas (write 1000 not 1,000)
 ➤ mixed numbers (such as $2\frac{1}{2}$, which must be gridded as 5/2 or 2.5).

RECOMMENDATION: ALWAYS START YOUR ANSWER IN THE FIRST COLUMN BOX

Technically, you can start in any column, but follow this rule to avoid mistakes. Do so even if your answer has only one or two figures. If you always start with the first column, your answers will always fit. Since there is no oval for 0 in the first column, grid an answer of 0 in any other column.

Note: If your answer is .7, don't grid 0.7! You can't grid a 0 in the first column.

Start your answer in the first column box whenever possible.

IN A FRACTIONAL ANSWER, GRID (/) IN THE CORRECT COLUMN

The sign (/) separates the numerator from the denominator. It appears only in columns two and three.

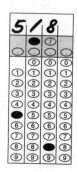

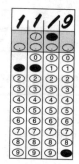

Example: If you get an answer of 5/8. Grid (/) in column two.

Example: If you get an answer of 11/9. Grid (/) in column three.

Warning: *A fractional answer with four digits — like 31/42 won't fit.*

CHANGE MIXED NUMBERS TO DECIMALS OR FRACTIONS BEFORE YOU GRID

If you try to grid a mixed number, it will be read as a fraction, and be counted wrong. For example, 4 1\2 will be read as the fraction 41\2, which is $20 \frac{1}{2}$.

So first change mixed numbers to fractions or decimals, then grid in. In this case:

➤ change 4 1\2 to 9\2 and grid in the fraction as shown below;

➤ or change $4\frac{1}{2}$ to 4.5 and grid in the decimal.

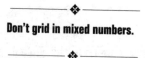

Don't grid in mixed numbers.

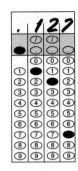

WATCH WHERE YOU PUT YOUR DECIMAL POINTS

➤ For a decimal less than 1, such as .127, enter the decimal point in the first box, as shown in the figure above.

➤ Only put a 0 before the decimal point if it's part of the answer, as in 20.5 — don't put one there (if your answer is, say, .5) just to make your answer look more accurate.

➤ Never grid a decimal point in the last column.

WITH LONG OR REPEATING DECIMALS, GRID THE FIRST THREE DIGITS ONLY AND PLUG IN THE DECIMAL POINT WHERE IT BELONGS

➤ Say three answers are .45454545, 82.452312, and 1.428743. Grid .454, 82.4, and 1.42 respectively.

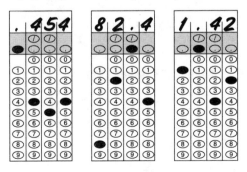

➤ You could round 1.428743 up to the nearest hundredth (1.43). Since it's not required, though, don't bother rounding off: You could make a mistake. Note that rounding to an even shorter answer — 1.4 — would be incorrect.

❖

Be careful with decimals. As a rule, don't round off.
Just chop off the excess digits.

❖

ON GRID-INS WITH MORE THAN ONE RIGHT ANSWER, CHOOSE ONE AND ENTER IT.

Say you're asked for a two-digit integer that is a multiple of 2, 3, and 5. You might answer 30, 60, or 90. Whichever you grid would be right.

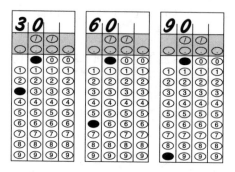

SOME GRID-INS HAVE A RANGE OF POSSIBLE ANSWERS

Suppose you're asked to grid a value of m where $1 - 2m < m$ and $5m - 2 < m$. Solving for m in the first inequality, you find that $\frac{1}{3} < m$. Solving for m in the second inequality, you find that $m < \frac{1}{2}$. So $\frac{1}{3} < m < \frac{1}{2}$. Grid in any value between $\frac{1}{3}$ and $\frac{1}{2}$. (Gridding in $\frac{1}{3}$ or $\frac{1}{2}$ would be wrong.) When the answer is a range of values, it's often easier to work with decimals: .333 < m < .5. Then you can quickly grid .4 (or .35 or .45, etc.) as your answer.

---❖---

Don't be thrown by Grid-ins that have a range of possible answers; choose one and grid it in.

---❖---

WRITE YOUR ANSWERS IN THE NUMBER BOXES

This doesn't get you points by itself, but you will make fewer mistakes if you write your answers in the number boxes. You may think that gridding directly will save time, but writing first, then gridding, helps ensure accuracy, which means more points.

---❖---

Unless you're almost out of time, don't try to save time by gridding without writing in the numbers first. (But make sure you do fill in the ovals.)

---❖---

Grid-in Pop Quiz

(Note: This quiz tests only your gridding ability. On the actual SAT, you'll have to do a regular math problem, get the answer, and then grid it in. But here, we've already given you the answers to grid. Just fill out the grids to reflect the answers given.)

126    $\frac{3}{8}$ 85.9   2,143 $5\frac{1}{2}$

0   .141414 $\frac{14}{5}$ $1\frac{2}{3}$ 8.175

Gridding Answers

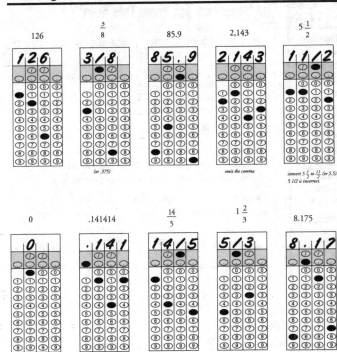

126

$\frac{3}{8}$
(or .375)

85.9

2,143
omit the comma

$5\frac{1}{2}$
convert $5\frac{1}{2}$ to $\frac{11}{2}$ (or 5.5).
5 1/2 is incorrect.

0

.141414
place the decimal point in the 1st column and grid as many digits as possible.

$\frac{14}{5}$

$1\frac{2}{3}$
convert $1\frac{2}{3}$ to $\frac{5}{3}$ (or 1.66 or 1.67). 12/3 is incorrect.

8.175
(or 8.18). Start in the left column and grid as many digits as possible.

Step 13 Recap: Grid-in Techniques

The Important Tips From This Step

➤ You can only get a point if you correctly fill in the ovals below the boxes.

➤ Make sure you grid in only one oval per column.

➤ Start your answer in the first column box whenever possible.

➤ Don't grid in mixed numbers.

➤ Be careful with decimals. As a rule, don't round off. Just chop off the excess digits.

➤ Don't be thrown by Grid-ins that have a range of possible answers; choose one and grid it in.

➤ Unless you're almost out of time, don't try to save time by gridding without writing in the numbers first. (But make sure you do fill in the ovals).

Step 14: End-of-Time Techniques

A CORRECT GUESS IS WORTH AS MUCH AS ANY OTHER CORRECT ANSWER

Obviously, the best way to find an answer is to actually solve the problem in the normal way. But if you're stuck or running out of time at the end of a section, shortcuts and guessing can be good alternatives.

All SAT questions except Grid-ins are scored to discourage random guessing. For every question you get right you earn a whole point. For every question you get wrong, you lose a fraction of a point. So if you guess at random on a number of questions, the points you gain from correct guesses are theoretically canceled out by the points you lose on incorrect guesses, for no overall gain or loss.

But you *can* make educated guesses. This raises the odds of guessing correctly, so the fractional points you lose no longer cancel out all the whole points you gain. You have just raised your score.

To make an educated guess, eliminate answer choices you know to be wrong, and guess from what's left. Of course, the more answer choices you can eliminate, the better chance you have of guessing the correct answer from what's left over.

❖

If you can't answer a question, eliminate what choices you can, and then guess.

❖

Here are some strategies for getting quick points on Math and Verbal problems when you don't have time to really think them through.

☐ 1. ELIMINATING UNREASONABLE ANSWER CHOICES

Before you guess, think about the problem, and decide which answers don't make logical sense. Try this next problem.

EXAMPLE

The ratio of men to women in a certain room is 13:11. If there are 429 men in the room, how many women are there?

(A) 143

(B) 363

(C) 433

(D) 507

(E) 792

Solution:

➤ The ratio of men to women is 13:11, so there are more men than women.

➤ Since there are 429 men, there must be fewer than 429 women.

➤ So you can eliminate choices (C), (D), and (E).

➤ The answer must be either (A) or (B), so guess. The correct answer is (B).

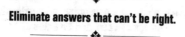

Eliminate answers that can't be right.

HINT: *Math answer choices are typically given in increasing or decreasing order, making it easier to eliminate some choices that are way off.*

❏ 2. ELIMINATING THE OBVIOUS ON HARD QUESTIONS

HINT: On harder questions, obvious answers are usually wrong.

On the hard questions (those that appear late in a set), obvious answers are usually wrong. So eliminate them when you guess. This rule of thumb doesn't hold true for early, easy questions, where the obvious answer is usually right.

Now apply the rule. In the following difficult problem, which obvious answer should you eliminate?

EXAMPLE

A number x is increased by 30% and then the result is decreased by 20%. What is the final result of these changes?

(A) x is increased by 10%

(B) x is increased by 6%

(C) x is increased by 4%

(D) x is decreased by 5%

(E) x is decreased by 10%

Solution:

If you picked (A) as the obvious choice to eliminate, you'd be right. Most people would combine the decrease of 20% with the increase of 30%, getting a net increase of 10%. That's the easy, obvious answer, but not the correct answer. If you must guess, avoid (A). The correct answer is (C).

❖

**Eliminate easy, obvious answers on hard questions
(those that appear late in a set).**

❖

This strategy also applies to Vocabulary-in-Context questions in Critical Reading. The most familiar definition of a word is rarely correct, so, in a time pinch, eliminate it.

EXAMPLE

In line 45, "temper" most nearly means

(A) disposition
(B) nature
(C) anger
(D) mood
(E) mixture

Even without reading the passage, you can guess that the right answer won't be (C), since that is the "obvious" answer.

☐ 3. EYEBALLING LENGTHS, ANGLES, AND AREAS ON GEOMETRY PROBLEMS

Use diagrams that accompany geometry problems to help you eliminate wrong answer choices. First make sure that the diagram is drawn to scale. If it is, estimate quantities or eyeball the diagram. Then eliminate answer choices that seem way too large or too small.

Diagrams are always drawn to scale unless there's a note like this: "Note: Figure not drawn to scale." If you see this note, don't use this strategy.

LENGTH

When a geometry question asks for a length, use the given lengths to estimate the unknown length. Measure off the given length by making a nick in your pencil with your thumbnail (you're not allowed to bring a ruler). Then hold the pencil against the unknown length on the diagram to see how the lengths compare.

In the following problem, which answer choices can you eliminate by eyeballing?

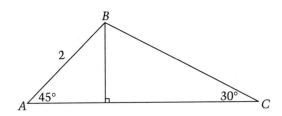

In the figure above, what is the length of *BC*?

(A) $\sqrt{2}$

(B) 2

(C) $2\sqrt{2}$

(D) 4

(E) $4\sqrt{2}$

Solution:

➤ *AB* is 2, so measure off this length on your pencil.

➤ Compare *BC* with this length.

➤ *BC* appears almost twice as long as *AB*, so *BC* is about 4.

➤ Since $\sqrt{2}$ is about 1.4, choices (A) and (B) are too small.

➤ Choice (E) is much greater than 4, so eliminate that.

➤ Now guess between (C) and (D). The correct answer is (C).

ANGLES

You can also eyeball angles. To eyeball an angle, compare the angle with a familiar angle, such as a straight angle (180°), a right angle (90°), or half a right angle (45°). The corner of your answer grid is a right angle, so use that to see if an angle is greater or less than 90° (but be careful not to make any stray marks on your answer grid!).

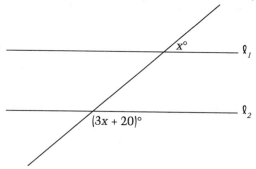

In the figure above, if line 1 ∥ line 2, what is the value of x?

(A)   130
(B)   100
(C)   80
(D)   50
(E)   40

Solution:

➤ You see that x is less than 90 degrees, so eliminate choices (A) and (B).

➤ Since x appears to be much less than 90 degrees, eliminate choice (C).

➤ Now pick between (D) and (E). In fact, the correct answer is (E).

AREAS

Eyeballing an area is similar to eyeballing a length. You compare an unknown area in a diagram to an area that you do know.

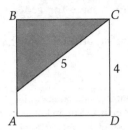

In square *ABCD* above, what is the area of the shaded region?

(A) 10

(B) 9

(C) 8

(D) 6

(E) 4

Solution:

➤ Since *ABCD* is a square, it has area 4^2, or 16.

➤ The shaded area is less than half the size of the square, so its area must be less than 8.

➤ Eliminate answer choices (A), (B), and (C). The correct answer is (D).

❖

Eyeball figures drawn to scale and eliminate answers that are way off.

❖

❑ 4. FINDING THE RANGE AND GUESSING ON GRID-INS

On Grid-ins, there are no answer choices to eliminate, but Grid-ins are the only questions on which you won't lose points for guessing wrong. So, if you're stuck, try to estimate the general range of the answer, and guess.

See if you can guess intelligently on the following hard Grid-in.

EXAMPLE

A triangle has one side of length 3 and another of length 7.
If the length of the longest side is a solution to the equation
$x^2 - 2x = 63$, what is the length of the longest side?

Solution:

Even if you can't solve that quadratic, you know that the sum of any two sides of a triangle must be greater than the length of the third side. So the third side must be less than $7 + 3$, or 10, but greater than 7 (since it is the longest side). Since solutions to SAT quadratics are usually integers, pick an integer between 7 and 10. If you picked 9, you'd be right.

❖

**Never leave a Grid-in blank. Find an approximate range
for the answer and guess. There's no penalty!**

❖

❑ 5. LOOKING FOR THE FAST POINTS IN CRITICAL READING

What do you do if you find yourself a minute from the end of a verbal section with one Critical Reading passage still totally unread? Skip the passage entirely and go for the quick points. Here's what you should look for:

Vocabulary-in-Context questions

These questions always have a line reference. Read the cited part of the passage and then decide which choice would be the best substitute for the keyed word.

Little Picture questions

Find the ones with specific line references. Read around the cited part of the passage and then answer the question as well as you can.

---- ❖ ----

If you don't have time to read a Critical Reading passage, skip the passage and try to answer the Vocabulary-in-Context questions first, then the Little Picture questions.

---- ❖ ----

Step 14 Recap: End-of-Time Techniques

The Important Tips From This Step

➤ If you can't answer a question, eliminate what choices you can, and then guess.

➤ Eliminate answers that can't be right.

➤ Eliminate easy, obvious answers on hard questions (those that appear late in a set).

➤ Eyeball figures drawn to scale and eliminate answers that are way off.

➤ Never leave a Grid-in blank. Find an approximate range for the answer and guess. There is no penalty!

➤ If you don't have time to read a Critical Reading passage, skip the passage and try to answer the Vocabulary-in-Context questions first, then the Little Picture Questions.

Step 15: Last-Minute Tips

AND NOW...THE SAT

Is it starting to feel like your whole life is a buildup to the SAT? You've known about it for years, worried about it for months, and now spent at least a few hours in solid preparation for it. As the test gets closer, you may find your anxiety is on the rise. You shouldn't worry. After the preparation you've received from this book, you're in good shape for test day.

To calm any pre-test jitters you may have, let's go over a few strategies for the couple of days before and after the test.

❑ THREE DAYS BEFORE THE TEST

If you've left yourself this much time, take a full-length practice test under timed conditions. This can be an actual published SAT or the test contained in the Kaplan Sneak Preview. If it's a full week before the test, you may even be able to go to the local Kaplan center to take a free diagnostic practice SAT. Call 1-800-KAP-TEST to find the Kaplan center nearest you.

Try to use all of the techniques and tips you've learned in this book. Approach the test strategically, actively, and confidently.

> WARNING: Don't take a full practice SAT if you have less than 48 hours left before the test. Doing so will probably exhaust you, hurting your scoring potential on the actual test! You wouldn't run a marathon the day before the real thing, would you?

❏ TWO DAYS BEFORE THE TEST

Go over the results of your practice test. Don't worry too much about your score or whether you got a specific question right or wrong. The practice test doesn't count, remember. But do examine your performance on specific questions with an eye to how you might get through each one faster and with greater accuracy on the actual test to come.

After reviewing your test, look over the "At-a-Glance" section at the beginning of each day's chapter. If you feel a little shaky about any of the topics mentioned, quickly read the relevant sections of the chapter.

---❖---

Use At-a-Glance boxes to guide your final studying.

---❖---

Do your last studying — read over the Quick Tips in the Step Recaps, review a couple of the more difficult principles we've covered, do a few more practice problems, and call it quits.

---❖---

Make sure you grasp the meaning of every Quick Tip in every Step Recap.

---❖---

❏ THE NIGHT BEFORE THE TEST

DON'T STUDY

Get together an "SAT survival kit" containing the following items:
➤ a calculator with fresh batteries
➤ a watch

- ➤ a few #2 pencils (pencils with slightly dull points fill the ovals better)
- ➤ erasers
- ➤ photo ID card
- ➤ your admission ticket from ETS
- ➤ a snack — there are two breaks and you'll probably get hungry

---

Assemble an "SAT survival kit."

Know exactly where you're going, exactly how you're getting there, and exactly how long it takes to get there. It's probably a good idea to visit your test center sometime before test day, so that you know what to expect — what the rooms are like, how the desks are set up, and so on.

Relax the night before the test. Read a good book, take a bubble bath, watch TV. Get a good night's sleep. Go to bed early and leave yourself extra time in the morning.

Don't study the night before the test.

❏ THE MORNING OF THE TEST

- ➤ Eat breakfast. Make it something substantial, but not anything too heavy or greasy.
- ➤ Don't drink a lot of coffee if you're not used to it; bathroom breaks cut into your time, and too much caffeine is a bad idea.
- ➤ Dress in layers so that you can adjust to the temperature of the test room.

❖

Dress in layers.

❖

➤ Read something. Warm up your brain with a newspaper or a magazine. You shouldn't let the SAT be the first thing you read that day.

❖

Warm up your brain by reading something.

❖

➤ Be sure to get there early. Allow yourself extra time for traffic, mass transit delays, and/or detours around people (like your old algebra teacher) who might only add to your stress level if you stopped to talk to them.

❏ DURING THE TEST

Don't be shaken. If you find your confidence slipping, remind yourself how well you've prepared. You know the structure of the test; you know the instructions; you've had practice with — and have learned strategies for — every question type.

Even if something goes really wrong, don't panic. If the test booklet is defective—two pages are stuck together or the ink has run— try to stay calm. Raise your hand and tell the proctor you need a new book. If you accidentally misgrid your answer page or put the answers in the wrong section, again *don't panic*. Raise your hand and tell the proctor. He or she might be able to arrange for you to re-grid your test after it's over, when it won't cost you any time.

❖

Be calm, systematic, and confident.
Remember: You've prepared for this test.

❖

Don't think about which section is experimental. Remember, you never know for sure which section won't count. Besides, you can't work on any other section during that section's designated time slot.

❖

Don't try to guess which section is experimental.

❖

❏ AFTER THE TEST

Once the test is over, put it out of your mind. If you don't plan to take the test again, shelve this book and start thinking about more interesting things.

You might walk out of the SAT thinking that you blew it. This is a normal reaction. Lots of people — even the highest scorers — feel that way. You tend to remember the questions that stumped you, not the many that you knew. If you're really concerned, call us for advice.

You can also call ETS within 24 hours to find out about canceling your score. But there is usually no good reason to do so. Remember, colleges typically accept your highest SAT score. And no test experience is going to be perfect. If you were distracted by the proctor's hacking cough this time around, next time you may be even more distracted by construction noise, or a cold, or the hideous lime-green sweater of the person sitting in front of you.

If, on the other hand, you had some real problems — a proctor who called time early, a testing room where the temperature hovered just below freezing — call us! We'll help you decide what to do. As a test-taker, you have certain rights. We'll help you make sure those rights aren't violated!

❖

**Don't cancel your score unless you have a good reason to.
But if you do have a good reason, call us.**

❖

**Remember, if you had any significant problems with your testing experience, or if
you just feel that, for reasons beyond your control, you didn't do as well as you
should have, call Kaplan at 1-800-KAP-TEST and we'll help!**

❏ POST-SAT FESTIVITIES

After all the hard work you've put in preparing for and taking the
SAT, you want to make sure you take time to celebrate afterward.
Plan to get together with friends the evening after the test. Relax,
have fun, let loose. After all, you've got lots to celebrate: You prepared for the test ahead of time. You did your best. You're going to get
a good score.

So start thinking about all of the great parties you'll be attending
at the college of your choice!

❖

Plan your SAT victory party.

❖

Step 15 Recap: Last-Minute Tips

The Important Tips From This Step

➤ Use the At-a-Glance boxes to guide your last studying.

➤ Make sure you grasp the meaning of every Quick Tip in every Step Recap.

➤ Assemble an "SAT Survival Kit."

➤ Don't study the night before the test.

➤ Dress in layers.

➤ Warm up your brain by reading something.

➤ Be calm, systematic, and confident. Remember: You've prepared for this test.

➤ Don't try to guess which section is experimental.

➤ Don't cancel your score unless you have a good reason, but if you do need to cancel, call us.

➤ Plan your SAT victory party.

Afterword

Well, you're finished. You've done just about all you can do in a week to prepare for the SAT. By now you should feel confident of your ability to perform well on the test. Even with just a week or so of preparation under your belt, you're still far more prepared than most SAT takers.

But we at Kaplan want you to know that our obligation to you doesn't stop with this book. Kaplan is a test-prep organization with extensive resources, and we are firmly committed to supporting our students on a long-term basis. After all, we've helped more than 1.5 million students score their best on standardized tests.

So, if you need more help, or if you just want to know more about the SAT, college admissions, or Kaplan prep courses for the PSAT, SAT, and ACT, give us a call at 1-800-KAP-TEST. We're here to answer your questions and to help you in any way we can.

Notes